I'm Not The Pastor's Wife

(I'm just married to him)

Natalia Peterson

12/13/13

To Joni—
Embrace your
authenticity!

Natalia
Peterson
a.k.a.

Talia

ISBN: 1492766836
ISBN 13: 9781492766834
Library of Congress Control Number: 2013919465
CreateSpace Independent Publishing Platform
North Charleston, South Carolina

For more information on the author or book orders please visit nataliapeterson.org

To crazy ol' Maurice

Contents

Prologue

I am one of the world's biggest brats and I adopt that title with pride. I don't believe anyone who knows me thinks I'm malicious; I'm betting people know that behind the twinkle in my eye is a person whose wheels are rolling on figuring out how to upset the apple cart either to make a statement or for a bit of amusement.

I'm happily at a point in my life where I no longer am focusing on child-rearing-please-God-make-sure-none-of-the-kids-becomes-incarcerated. Anyone who has blended a family with three teenagers would completely understand that a person's time is consumed with: A) Doing the thing you believe is right at the moment; and B) Praying your kids stay happy, healthy, productive members of society, and won't need lifetime therapy to undo the mistakes you've made raising them.

Now that my husband and I are empty-nesters, hard as it may be we've needed to let our little birds fly. That also meant I needed a new purpose, or if nothing better, a new hobby.

Most times when I'd felt this sort of restlessness, I would tap into my talent and educational pool. Having studied music and some theatre in college, I'd find a creative project that used those particular skills.

I tried getting excited about writing music again, but nothing creative was coming out of my head onto manuscript paper. Everything I wrote sounded so trite I considered playwriting might be a good idea.

No luck there either. Plot twists just weren't happening for me.

The thought of writing a screenplay about a family member with an amazing life story had been in the back of my mind for at least two decades. A screenwriter advised me to start with a book first, as Hollywood wasn't simply going to pick up a script from an unknown screenwriter and gamble millions of dollars on it.

Write a book? How absurd. My college professors could attest that my writing skills were average at best, at least when it came to writing research papers. Realizing it would take up to five years to gather the research needed for the book-turned-screenplay, I had some reservations. I don't have five years of patience for anything.

Nevertheless, I was undaunted. I'd always been a reasonable storyteller, and I figured, what I lacked in knowledge of good grammar and punctuation could be rectified by an editor. The big question was – what was I going to write about?

I sat contemplatively on my couch and looked at my husband. He was busy with his usual Saturday night ritual.

Sorry to say, it wasn't an effort to have a romantic escapade with me. Saturday nights were work nights for him and he would more than likely be thinking about work in his sleep, as well. He was writing his sermon for Sunday worship at the church he was serving at as senior pastor.

When I announced my engagement to a pastor back in the year 2000, I received a few strange looks, but mostly a lot of gut-splitting laughter. Being mischievous as well as being married to a pastor is usually thought of as being an oxymoron to most people. Once, after I took a series of behavior and personality tests, a counselor in personality profiling stared at my scores and charts, looked at me with a puzzled eye and asked, "Has anyone ever told you that you're unconventional?"

"Yes," I replied through my laughter, "though most people have just used the word brat."

As I watched my husband write his sermon I thought back to my session with that counselor and wondered how I ever managed to marry a man who was so focused, as well as believed in something that had always been a conundrum for me – God and religion.

He glanced my way. "What is it?"

"What is what?"

"Why are you looking at me that way?"

"What way?"

"You know what way. You have trouble written all over your face."

Trouble, indeed. I could feel my impish smirk surfacing. I left the room and went online on my own computer to see if anything had been written about the subject I began considering for my book. It appeared that the literary world hadn't been saturated by it.

I thought about the congregation who would be listening to his sermon the next day. Most of them were such lovely people, yet way too often they'd make a certain remark that *really* irked me:

I'm at church and one of my friends of the congregation has brought a guest. This friend comes up to me and makes introductions.

"This is my friend so-and-so, and this is 'The Pastor's Wife.'"

I drive twenty minutes to the home fix-it store and I see a congregation member who hails me down. We talk amiably for a few minutes and someone he knows walks by and he says hi to his friend. He then turns to him and introduces me. "This is 'The Pastor's Wife' at my church."

I visit my in-laws and attend their church on a Sunday. Someone stops my husband and welcomes him back home. This person looks at me and says, "You're his wife, right? What was your name again?"

Does all courtesy fly out the window when you marry a pastor? Suddenly I had no name, no occupation and no identity of my own.

Granted, I was given an unusual name to remember in the land of one million Scandinavians of Minnesota: I was baptized Natal'ya Mariya Makovets'ka. I won't even attempt to explain the contortions your mouth has to go through to pronounce the consonants in my name followed by an apostrophe.

My name, of course, was not written this way on my birth certificate. My parents wouldn't have been that cruel to me. Natalie Mary Makowesky was the name with which I was branded. People came up with a plethora of names to identify me: Nat, Natty, Natalia, Natalka, Gnat with the "g" pronounced for two years in junior high school, Bratalie, and my favorite, Talia. My entire life people have known who I was simply because no other Natalie or Natalia crossed their paths.

I'd also been known as a singer, pianist, composer, actor, public speaker, playwright, director, print model, the person whose voice you hear over some boring industrial video – all these creative gifts worked on and fostered for decades – yet now I was relegated to the passenger seat of my husband's profession as "The Pastor's Wife." About a year ago I began retorting to this archaic introduction by saying, "I'm not 'The Pastor's Wife'; I'm just married to him."

It sounded like a great title for a book.

Perhaps you, dear reader, have never stepped into a house of worship of any kind. Doesn't matter. Just transfer the word "church" to any other institution and you'll be nodding your heads saying, "Oh, yeah, I've been there." This type of introduction will more than likely be empathized by Military Officer's Wives, Doctor's Wives and the First Ladies of the United States.

When I told my husband of my book title, he asked me why I didn't title the book, *I'm Not The Pastor's Spouse,* since some men are married to female pastors.

Guess what? The rules are different. A woman can have her own career, but if she doesn't attend her husband's church or doesn't volunteer in any way, she's not supportive. For a man married to a pastor, he's naturally supporting his family and probably involved with very important responsibilities somewhere else. Why would there be any gossip about his absence? Face it, everyone, women have come a long way but we have far to go before equality is truly equality.

Being a person who has a difficult time saying no to an adventure completely foreign to me (much to my husband's chagrin), I pulled out the computer keyboard instead of the ivories and got cracking. I also enrolled in a writing course that focused on creative non-fiction.

I had a wonderful instructor who allowed us to submit work for her to critique. My initial instincts were right; I was a good story-teller and dreadful at grammar and punctuation. The book started out as a tongue-in-cheek look of the idiosyncrasies of church life and what it's like being married to a pastor.

I wrote about four chapters and then there was nothing else to write about. I realized no one would read a thirty page book.

As the class continued, my instructor kept encouraging us to do what is called discovery writing –writing about anything that comes to mind. As I handed in some of my discovery work to her, I would, naturally, receive my manuscript filled with corrections. What I didn't expect was her opinion that the story of my life might be something people would be interested in reading. She'd write things in the margins, such as, "keep going this direction," or "I can visualize what you're writing," and her favorite phrase, "go for the ache."

Well, the ache was what I got. No one said spilling out your life for anyone who cares to read about it was going to be easy.

There really is nothing unusual about my life. My story is everyone's story. Mine will have different characters and circumstances than yours, but the truth is, in the hilarious, tragic, or even in the common moments, most writers can't make up stuff more entertaining or heart-wrenching than that which occurs in real life

I do offer you this warning: To keep everything true to life, this book is written without any suppression of colorful language. Just because the word "pastor" is in the title doesn't mean it's squeaky clean. It definitely wouldn't be appropriate to catalogue this piece of literature under the "Religion" section in a bookstore. "Autobiographical Tragicomedy," or possibly, "Abnormal Psychology" might be better categories. So if you don't want any of your kids picking it up and reading some PG-13 cussing and swearing, put it in the same place you keep your steamy romance novels.

Or go ahead and leave it out for them to read. It might be valuable for them to know you gotta be a little nuts if you're going to be The Pastor's Wife.

Keep Your Eye on the Ball

Growing up in a neighborhood full of boys, my one and only girlfriend and I ended up playing softball for summer entertainment. I was a glutton for punishment since my performance in any sport was and is dreadful, but what else are you going to do for three months over the summer without getting into trouble? Everyone played to win and no pitcher passively threw the ball just to make me feel good about myself and let me hit it. The most infuriating part for me when I came up to bat was watching everyone move in from the outfield. It's bad enough not being able to hit the ball regularly; when your infield doubles on defense, it's nearly impossible to get on base.

Once in a while the entire neighborhood dropped their jaws when by happenstance I would swing and hit the ball past the diamond. I'd get so thrilled the bat would fling out of my hands and on more than one occasion it whacked the catcher in the head. Quite hard – actually – sometimes drawing blood.

Since my depth perception is skewed when attempting to hit anything faster than a badminton birdie, I knew even back then I had to develop a skill outside of batting to keep playing with the guys. I began to work on my pitching.

By high school, I did develop one good pitch. I would throw the ball perfectly into the strike zone and just as it approached the batter, it would suddenly drop. It was my own variation of a curve ball, although it was more like a right-angle sinker. Nobody could time their swings accurately. There was no greater thrill for me than watching a bunch of teenaged boys swearing because the unathletic girl struck them out.

There's a reason the term "getting thrown a curveball" is used as a metaphor for an unexpected turn of events in life. Over the years I never anticipated those sneaky little throws coming at me, so I learned to swing quickly, jump out of the way or I would get smacked. By nature I'm not afraid to take risks; that, of course exacerbates life's little curveballs and in some way I was going to have to learn how to deal with them. Example:

After college I was dating a journalist working on a national political campaign and he was hired to work as press secretary for a newly elected U.S. representative in Washington, D.C. I was just beginning my fine arts career in the Twin Cities of Minneapolis and St. Paul, Minnesota. The night before he left for D.C., he said, "I think we should get married."

Curveball. Whoa – didn't see that one coming.

I said yes. Swing and a hit.

Four years later, we were raising a one-year-old daughter, and practically overnight our marriage fell apart.

WHOA – that curveball I absolutely did *not* see coming.

I was smacked right in the heart and launched on the ground. I became single again and moved back to St. Paul, the only place I could really call home.

I was parenting as a single mother and frankly enjoyed my singlehood. I dated more than I ever had before I was married and could come and go as I pleased. I bought a little house, had fun with my little girl, was able to juggle several part-time jobs around her school schedule and was content with my comfortable little life. I wasn't looking for a partner. I was happy with the way things were. I had no plans to marry again as I hadn't found wedded bliss all that it was cracked up to be.

I had been single for twelve years when the Grand Pitcher threw the ball at me again. I discovered someone who was worth the chance of a swing. It still took me two years to gather up the courage to hit the ball, but I eventually took that leap of faith. I swung and cracked that ball into a home run and gained two additional RBIs. I married a wonderful man, Charlie, a widowed Lutheran pastor with two sons. He was on leave of absence from parish ministry to raise his children. With my daughter as the middle child of this blended family, the kids were fourteen, fifteen and sixteen at the time of our wedding.

Sound crazy? We were either insane or hopelessly in love with each other. I believe we were a little of both.

My new husband and I were in total bliss with our marriage. Our children however, made it quite apparent that their lives had been turned upside-down. The boys were uprooted from their home town in Wisconsin to move to Minnesota and my daughter had to share me with someone else. Brooding became the standard emotion, which, let's be serious, would have been no different even if we were a nuclear family, considering the precarious ages of our children.

Going from two people to five overnight was a shock. Imagine my surprise when my grocery bill quadrupled at the very least and the cute little house for two females couldn't hold a half week's groceries with three extra men, all of them well above six feet in height. We could all feel the place splitting at the seams, so a bigger home in a different neighborhood became our main priority. Starting brand new for everyone was one of the smarter moves we made. Even the three cats we blended could settle into their own new territories and we no longer saw tufts of animal hair scattered from their tussles.

To cover the expenses of raising three teenagers I began working a full-time management job in marketing. Charlie found a full-time job outside of the Church and was also taking master's-level classes in marriage and family therapy. He wasn't sure he wanted to go back into parish ministry, but he did want to stay connected in some way ministering to people.

A couple years into our marriage my husband received a phone call from his former bishop, letting him know that a half-time position as an interim pastor had opened up in Wisconsin, just across the border. The job would last a year or so.

Would it work? He would be gone about three days a week, work part-time at his other job and finish his master's all at once.

*Hmm...*I was dubious about the prospect with me gone all day at work and three teenagers to keep track of. We talked with the kids, explained to them if Charlie was to take on this interim position they would need to kick it up a notch with household responsibilities and self-sufficiency.

Sure, that's no problem, we're not little kids anymore, we can take care of ourselves, blah, blah, blah...

Kids will tell you anything you want to hear.

The house became a disaster. Dishes were left in every room, each child's bedroom harbored at least a month's worth of laundry and their assigned household chores were not getting done. My husband had the schedule of a medical school intern and I was unconvincingly reassuring myself about the situation by repeating, "We did the right thing...we did the right thing...omygod, did we do the right thing?"

I finally decided to ignore the clutter and muck and picked my battles. Their laundry became their responsibilities and with every family member flying in different directions, sit-down dinners meant grabbing what was available and sitting down – right in front of the TV.

Okay, so the 1950s sit-com family we were not.

A year had passed when we received another phone call. It was a woman I'd known since childhood. Her congregation was looking for a full-time pastor, and would my husband be interested? It was located in a sleepy little community, thirty-five miles away from our suburban home and eventually we would need to live there. Our youngest was just finishing his junior year of high school and we weren't willing to move him again. Charlie and I talked it over and decided if he was offered the job he would commute until our youngest graduated.

Finally, in the late fall of 2004, my husband received a call to embark on a journey to serve as senior pastor in a church community that was very Swedish and very Lutheran. The congregation was excited, as they would be welcoming a new Pastor and the woman he was married to, despite the fact she had been...well... you know... that "D" word... seemed morally acceptable.

I was thrown a curveball I had never experienced before nor ever anticipated in my life.

I was going to be The Pastor's Wife

The Pastor's Wife

For anyone who has been raised in a mainstream white Protestant church during most of the twentieth century, there was more than likely a woman hanging around known as The Pastor's Wife. The Pastor's Wife was quite visible along with her ordained husband. The Pastor's Wife played the organ, sang in the choir, taught Sunday school, headed up baking fund-raisers, held Bible studies and to keep the congregation running, took on all the jobs in the church no one else wanted to do. Her house was "white glove test" clean at all times, especially if she lived in a parsonage, which is a house provided by the church and was usually next door. This gave her the pleasure of receiving unexpected visits at any given time of day. She was always ready to entertain the parishioners with fresh coffee and an array of desserts, including those baked with saccharin for people who needed to keep a watch on their blood-sugar levels.

The Pastor's Wife also raised anywhere from two to six children, and for the most part on her own due to The Pastor's fifty-plus-hour-a-week schedule. The family scored points if at least one or two of the children were not biological but adopted, even more points if the child was from Asia or Latin America to provide a much- needed home for a child from an under-privileged environment. Adopting from Africa or any country whose population were descendents from that continent would have been too progressive. With the onset of civil rights actions for African-Americans in the 1960's, segregation and racism were still alive in many white Protestant churches.

The Pastor's Wife did not work outside the home unless she was a school teacher, so she could be available during The Pastor's Kids' (PKs') school breaks. It was especially important to be around in the summer to invariably host the congregation's children for mothers who had appointments or needed to take care of domestic errands and besides, what's one or two more children running around that big old parsonage anyway? How much trouble could your kid get into if they were friends with the PKs?

As for her personal sense of style it was important for The Pastor's Wife to convey to the congregation a neatly groomed look, but not too modern or expensive lest the parishioners might think they're over-paying The Pastor. Skirts or jumpers were always a good choice as they could be worn with long sleeves in the winter and short in the summer. One or two tailored suits were acceptable to have for group meetings or women's conferences, where a pair of high pumps would come out of their box. This was a nice diversion from the usual flats or low pumped heels that gathered many miles on them due to the chaotic nature of Sunday mornings. As for hair, it was acceptable to keep it dyed as long as it was a color found in nature and was purchased at the drug store and applied at home. The style would be coiffed so it was fashionable for the times as well as the two decades prior.   The Saturday night before worship she would furiously scrub her fingernails with paint thinner to remove the dye and file down her nails in case she was needed to play the organ or accompany the Sunday school children on the piano.

Sunday mornings The Pastor's Wife was "on" just as much as her husband. She attempted to maintain her husband's focus by giving him uninterrupted time in the morning to rehearse his sermon in front of the bathroom mirror as she wiped the breakfast off the faces of her children with her spit and handkerchief and made sure shirttails were tucked into pants or skirts. Once at church she made conversation with the parishioners, in particular with those who were prone to talk The Pastor's ear off. She seamlessly diverted their attention while he was trying to prepare for the service.

When the hour arrived for worship to begin, The Pastor's Wife would check the belfry to see if someone had remembered to ring the bell announcing The Pastor would be at the altar ready for the liturgy. If the belfry was empty, her low-heeled Sunday shoes came in quite handy to run up the precarious flights of stairs, ring the bell, and run back down to the sanctuary in complete control without showing a hint of being short winded. She would then fly into an up-front pew with her two to six impeccably behaved children who were there on time every single Sunday, without exception, to set a good example. It was important for all of the children to be attentive as traditionally at least half of them would become pastors or marry one.

The Pastor's Wife was a tremendous cook, seamstress, quilter, knitter, decorator, crafts maker and had the remarkable ability to stop children's wails during the service just by giving them the eye. She was always cheerful, social, knew everyone by name, and kept the strength of the coffee at church at a conservative level because as you know, coffee doesn't just grow on trees. She kept her politics to herself and when not volunteering at church she was planning her next Bible study and memorizing scripture. Her language remained clean, and if she even thought of a four-letter-word she chastised herself with an appropriate guilt trip.

As a child attending Roman Catholic school through the sixth grade, "The Pastor's Wife" was an oxymoron to me. The friends I had in my neighborhood were almost exclusively Protestant and none of them had a father who was a pastor. It wasn't until I attended a small Norwegian/Lutheran college in rural Minnesota in the late 1970s and early 1980s where I heard the terms "PW" (pastor's wife) and "PK" in normal, everyday conversation.

Upon my arrival at college I was pleasantly surprised that the pastoral intern was a young woman. I thought, "Wow! This Lutheran thing is pretty progressive!" In regards to a pastor's family life, however, many students at my college were PKs and their tales of growing up in a Lutheran church community illustrated to me the rigor of having a pastor for a dad and a pastor's wife for a mom. Some women broke the mold, but for the most part the protocol was adhered to by their mothers.

After meeting many of these lovely women who made this strong commitment to their families and their husbands' call, I came to a conclusion: The Pastor's Wife was a job of its own. A job I envisioned was not up my alley. I was too independent, too liberal and too insubordinate. I tried sitting through a Bible study once in college, but I became very antsy as everyone else in the room had this weird spiritual glow about them I just wasn't feeling. And as time progressed, I wasn't even sure organized religion was something in which I wanted to be involved.

SURPRISE! I became The Pastor's Wife.

For the record, these are my qualifications for the job:

I can sing and play piano.

I am social.

Things that do not qualify me for the job:

Everything else.

Unusual beginnings

It is mid-afternoon. In the living room sits a very pregnant woman, admiring the items of baby wear, diapers and newborn necessities. Her thoughts go back to her last doctor's visit:

"Do you have any idea if I'll be having a girl or a boy?" She pressed her doctor for some telltale sign. The doctor hesitated.

"There's no sure way to know."

She impishly nudged him for an answer. "But you have a hunch, don't you?"

The doctor had come to know this woman well as she had been a patient of his twice before. Both of those children were boys. He hemmed and hawed as her eyes twinkled. Her smile and endearing manner made it difficult not to be charmed by her.

"Alright, I'm telling you this but you need to remember that the medical profession is simply making a guess based on a common trend, so don't take my words as the truth. You got that?" She nodded her head, keeping her excitement to herself. "Indicated by the rapid heartbeat...now remember, I'm not making any accurate predictions...you just *might* be having a girl this time."

She rushed into the lobby all excited to tell her husband. She was thrilled that there would be a gender mix among the three children. While driving home, her husband kept informing her that doctors don't know for sure, so let's not go painting the bedroom pink yet.

In his own mind, however, he had an intuition that this time the child would be a girl. He had a sixth sense about certain things and the premonition was strong. Nevertheless, he kept it to himself just to be on the safe side.

His wife was not as cautious and told her best friend the doctor's "news." The gossip chain made its way around. The following Sunday, a baby shower was scheduled, as the youngest boy was only twenty months old and if nothing else, many more cloth diapers would be needed. Someone took a risk and bought a baby dress.

She pulls herself out of her reverie. She and her husband had been through so much already in their young lives and they are grateful for two healthy boys and a good third pregnancy. Several strong kicks inside her remind her that this one might be a handful. All of a sudden a pain seizes her, severe, taking her breath away. It comes back in five minutes. The woman is watching the clock and keeping aware of the time in between every two contractions. Two more. Four minutes. It's time to call her husband at work. He races home and the other two children are scurried across the street to a neighbor's house. In a mad dash they are on their way to the hospital. Another contraction rips through the woman.

Oh dear God, I'm going to have this one in the car.

The husband drops her off at the hospital while an attending nurse throws her in a wheelchair and whisks her inside. He parks the car and hastily makes his way to the maternity ward. Barely able to catch his own breath he is about to sit down in the reception area when out the door pops an unknown doctor, as the woman's own physician couldn't make it in time.

"Mr. Makowesky, you have a daughter."

Despite the profound fact that he and his wife have brought a new life into the world a strange thought crosses his mind.

Thank God we don't have to figure out what to do with that damn dress.

✳◉✳

My life began with drama and it has never stopped. I may have been a skinny five-and-a-half pound newborn, but I had a wail like a fire engine and I was ready to see the world. I was attracted to people, sounds, smells, pretty lights and from the get-go, I was an animated and dramatic child.

For my mom, having a girl was like having a little doll to play with. Dresses found at the least expensive stores were accessorized with lacy socks, frilly gloves and bonnets and other fashionable ways to make my flyaway hair look presentable. I was captivated by any new face and though I'm not sure why, adult men were my favorite people to be around as a baby. I'm guessing the smell of Brylcream my dad and all his friends used intrigued me, as did their deep soothing voices. I was never afraid of people and I could easily captivate them with my smiles, giggles and receptive hugs.

This stage lasted only as long as I was unable to talk. After uttering my first words I became incorrigible. Stubborn and mouthy was my conduct at home. My brothers bore most of the wicked behavior I doled out. My parents didn't know what to do with me. Spanking did no good, as I would casually say, "You can spank me all you want. It doesn't hurt me anyway."

I was a monster.

In public, however, I could play the darling card on cue. As much as it probably would have insulted my mom to hear this I was simply following her lead. She may have only been 4'9" tall and ninety pounds but she had a feisty side we as little kids didn't want to mess with. On the other hand she was normally very congenial by nature. She knew almost everyone on our neighborhood block by name and never hesitated to invite someone over for coffee or to chat for hours on the phone.

I adored being raised by my mom. I loved the fact that she would dress up the dining room table with her best china, even if it was just for an afternoon snack with a guest. I loved it when people would look down at her (literally) and called her by the diminutive name of "Annie," told her how little and cute she was and then I'd watch her go into action. She hated being short. She'd straighten up and show her authoritative determination, letting them know in a roundabout way that her height did not define her strength of character. I loved listening to her sing me to sleep and later teach me how to harmonize to a song.

I especially loved dressing up with her with our hats and purses and gloves and taking the bus downtown to run errands. We'd sit at the dime store counter and while she drank coffee, I insisted that my lemonade or hot chocolate be put in a cup just like hers. From the counter we would people watch. We would create stories about them. She would make impudent remarks about those imaginative lives that would split my sides into laughter.

As for my dad, he was pretty much like all other dads during the late 1960s – worked eight hours, five days a week at a physical job, came home to dinner, watched the news, and then took care of the outdoor chores. On a beautiful summer night he would lie on the squeaky porch glider and listen to the Minnesota Twins baseball game on the radio. In the winter it was North Stars hockey. Most kids never got much of a chance to bond with their dads in those days. Yet during the quiet moments of listening to sports, I could squeeze up next to him, his presence always making me feel secure. We didn't have to say a word to each other. I had the comfort of snuggling with him and the smell of Brylcream would still be wafting with me as I went to bed.

As I became older it didn't take me long to figure out that our family was different from all the others in our neighborhood. We spoke a foreign language with our parents, and it wasn't a common one. It was Ukrainian and at that time Ukraine was part of the Soviet Union. The Cold War and Communism were fears instilled in every American and some people, in their ignorance, would use hurtful language towards our family.

For many years as I was growing up, I wished that our family was normal. Normal to me was parents who could speak English without a funny accent. Wishing our heritage had no connections to Communism. Just once having a person look at my last name and pronounce it correctly. Knowing who my cousins were, to get to know them, to play with them, and not just turn the globe around to point to an area named Ukrainian S.S.R. and dream of someday meeting them.

It wasn't until I became an adult that my childhood friends told me they had coveted our lives. We had parents who engaged in conversation with them. We had a sense of heritage with roots that ran deep. They didn't know anyone else who spoke a foreign language, which was advantageous when my brothers and I played as a team against the neighborhood kids in football, calling out plays in Ukrainian to keep them guessing. It amazed our neighborhood that my parents never had any formal education beyond sixth grade due to the ravages of World War II in Eastern Europe, and yet somehow managed their way across the Atlantic to eventually become citizens of the United States with no prior knowledge of the English language. They truly did the best they could, mistakes and all. Over time it was apparent to me that my brothers and I could have been raised by parents who were much worse than ours.

As I grew up I also realized they didn't do it alone. Despite our lack of kin nearby, our family and other Ukrainians had help. A community was formed in a cold, rickety old building with a basement that leaked copious amounts of water after every rainfall and left a person smelling like a combination of wet, musty air and the incense that was burned during worship on Sunday mornings. It was a place we kids both hated and loved: St. Stephen's Ukrainian Greek Catholic Church.

✖✖

In the early-1950s, the Twin Cities were composed of many Ukrainian immigrants displaced after World War II. The most practical way of meeting and making friends with other Ukrainians was through a church. A group of families living in St. Paul wanted to form their own congregation and in 1959 St. Stephen's Ukrainian Greek Catholic Church was established. During the height of its existence, the congregation was busting its doors with about sixty parishioners, most of them being the offspring of the founding members.

The priest that served the church was elderly and also a recent immigrant. He spoke very little English. Keeping with the tradition of the Ukrainian Greek Catholic Church in Europe, he had been married with two children and several grandchildren. His name was Father Leo Dorosh and a kinder or gentler man didn't exist in my life. St. Stephen's Church was our family and Father Dorosh was our honorary grandfather. Tall, grey-haired, stately yet approachable, he gave sermons from which our parents could glean wisdom while we children were totally clueless as to what he was saying. Half the Ukrainian words he spoke were a mystery to me. It didn't matter. His tone was soft and caring and even if I didn't understand his message, I understood the goodness of the man.

The Sacrament of Confession was something we kids in the parish couldn't sneak away from. We were required by our parents to attend twice a year, before Christmas and Easter, whether we needed to or not. When going to Confession it wasn't all that easy to explain in Ukrainian all the horrible sins we'd committed that we thought would certainly be worthy of a considerable amount of time in purgatory. Father Dorosh listened to our butchered grammar and filled in words we couldn't think of off the tops of our heads. He then simply asked if we were sorry and gave us the standard three "Our Fathers" and three "Hail Marys" to pray for our penance and all was forgiven.

To make a few extra dollars my dad became the custodian of the church, which really meant about a two-hour clean-up during the week. My two brothers and I were often dragged along with him. We had to find something to do, and my youngest brother and I had great imaginations. We decided the confessional would be a great place to invent some spy mystery where we could whisper to each other through the panel. "Get Smart" was a popular TV show at the time and we built our espionage around the show's lampoons. We always made sure our dad was in the basement because in some unspoken way we knew playing spies in a confessional was in some way sacrilegious.

One Sunday my brother and I tiptoed upstairs after the church service while the rest of the congregation was in the basement. We checked to see if any other "spies" were watching as we entered our compartments of the confessional.

"This is Agent 44," he'd whisper.

"This is Agent 32," I'd respond, even more hushed.

"Have you got *'the secret papers'*?"

"I've got *'the secret papers'*."

"Take *'the secret papers'* across the street, go behind the lilac bush, walk to the next house, turn around the corner and agent 77 will meet you there."

"Roger, Agent 44. Over and out."

All of a sudden the confessional curtains were flung to the sides and my brother and I both gasped as if the KGB itself had caught us. I could feel my heartbeat racing and my blood pressure plummeting. There stood none other than the agency director himself, Father Dorosh.

Imagine two terrified kids, all the blood from their faces gone and eyes wide open with nothing coming out of their mouths.

Omygod, omygod, omygod, I would rather die right here and now and not have to experience the wrath of living hell for playing spies in the confessional. Please, God, just take me quickly and I'll spend a year in purgatory praying on my knees to make up for this.

Father Dorosh broke his stare at us and began chuckling, hugged us both and kept our rendezvous spot a secret. I was so freaked out by the situation I never dared to play in the confessional again and anytime I entered the space for its true purpose my heartbeat could be heard in my ears.

One never knew just what time worship would actually begin. Since Father Dorosh didn't drive, a rotation was set for a parishioner to pick him up from Minneapolis and drive him back home. The liturgy was to start at 10:00 a.m., but invariably he would get into a discussion with his chauffeur of the week and sometimes we would begin fifteen minutes late, sometimes thirty. Father Dorosh was a guy who would shoot the breeze with anyone and his flock was more important to him than punctuality. So to kill time we would all assemble ourselves in the church basement while the designated hostess for the after-church brunch would be setting up sandwiches, dessert and coffee until the five-minute-warning-bell rang.

After the service a good hour or so was spent eating, chatting, playing outdoors and when it was time to say good-bye to everyone it wouldn't be for long. In true Ukrainian fashion Sundays were made for entertaining. Unless the Minnesota weather was too cold, snowy, or the Minnesota Vikings were in the NFL play-offs or Super Bowl (a sacred and not-to-be-disturbed event for my dad), we would have company at our home or we'd jump in the car to go visit one of the families we had just seen at church.

Summers were great. The church congregation completely ditched the after-service brunches, quickly went home and grabbed swimsuits, towels and coolers. A half dozen or more families headed to a local beach. Throughout the day we ate too much, got sun burnt, became nauseous on the playground equipment and ingested too much lake water. We'd complain about our aches and pains and nausea on our drive home and our parents would yell into the backseat to quit whining. We'd pout from lack of sympathy. And then we'd get sick all over again the following week.

The St. Stephen's congregation was quite a demonstrative group, as are all Ukrainians. Girls would receive the benefit of hugs and pecks on the cheek from parish members. As they began maturing, boys got strong handshakes and loving pats on the back. And emotions! I can recall on more than one occasion seeing a table full of people in mournful tears, and the next moment cracking jokes. Heated debates about political candidates would raise voices, all the while a libation would be poured from a bottle. All arguments would then stop as someone bellowed *"Na zdorovya!"* and the adults shot down some sort of 90-proof liquid, knowing that nothing in the world, not even politics, could come between them. Sure, there was some bickering over inconsequential matters, but the Ukrainians I grew up with loved each other, for better or worse.

The one holiday that stood out among any other was Easter Sunday. When it came to fasting, the Roman Catholic regimen was tame compared to ours during Holy Week, the week between Palm Sunday and Easter. If you hadn't suffered quite enough from your regular lack of meat or dairy during Holy Week, Easter morning would be the killer. No food was eaten that morning as your first meal was to be blessed with holy water.

At 7:00 a.m., everyone was decked out in brand new suits, coats, dresses and shoes. We'd bring baskets full of meats, cheeses, breads and Easter eggs inside the church for the blessing. We sat through the three hour service with stomachs growling. And the smell! It was the most incredible gastronomic ensemble, reminding you just how starved you felt. All eyes were wide as Father Dorosh blessed the food that all of us would eat after the service.

A mad dash would ensue to get out of church to go eat with friends and family. The misery of hunger was eliminated as we all toasted, the adults with the 90- proof, the kids with shot glasses full of cheap Concord grape wine as the host would ring out *Christos Voskres!"** while the rest of the table would respond with *"Voyistono Voskres!"***

*Christ is Risen!"
**He is Risen, Indeed!

❈❂❈

Instead of having Sunday school of religious study, our Saturday mornings were consumed with Ukrainian school. We hated it. We were supposed to be educated on the language, history and culture of Ukraine. By the end of our eight years of "Uki" School, we knew how to read and write using the Cyrillic alphabet, were privy to a few geographical and historical details about Ukraine, and that's about all any of us can remember. I also learned about the curiosities and fundamentals of sex from one of my classmates. In actuality, the majority of our time was spent living out the dream of one particular woman, Mrs. Lucyk.

Mrs. Lucyk was a very passionate woman regarding art and culture. Her husband had died unexpectedly and she was left with two adult sons and a lot of time on her hands so she dedicated herself to making sure we children knew the beauty of our heritage. Every child was expected to memorize Ukrainian poetry and recite it with as much gusto as a king's proclamation. Traditional folk songs and plays written by her were rehearsed over and over until an occasion arose to perform them. So what if we couldn't quite understand the intricate grammar of the language? After every performance Mrs. Lucyk shed tears of sentimentality and joy knowing that each child could comprehend the depth of oppression Ukrainians had been under for so many centuries. For our performances we all wore our lovingly-made embroidered shirts, donning our patriotism.

Growing up with these Ukrainian immigrants and their children formed a foundation that was inexplicable to the Western Europeans in our neighborhoods, who were several generations removed from their immigrant ancestors. Sure, we whined when the liturgy was sung, adding an extra half hour to the service, or missed out on Saturday morning cartoons during Ukrainian school. As kids we often felt all this Ukrainian church stuff was a big pain in the ass. But kids are kids. I look back now and the significance of my youth in that musty basement is so obvious.

It was home.

The decades have passed, and the church that was once St. Stephen's is no longer in existence. Most of the founders have died and the offspring went in directions that were conducive to their own family lives. Knowing we'll never get headaches from the mold of the basement or the overpowering incense is actually quite bittersweet. St. Stephen's had a purpose. Our parents, who had no other family but each other, gave us the family we needed back in 1959. At St. Stephen's Ukrainian Greek Catholic Church we didn't learn much about theology, we simply followed our religious ancestry. We embraced our Ukrainian tradition and learned about loyalty to our church family with complete, unconditional love. I came to believe every church was like that.

Catholic School

Besides my St. Stephen's community, I was placed in another environment that fostered family-like ties. I was enrolled for six years at St. Patrick's Catholic Elementary School.

I had a positive experience attending St. Pat's. It was a good old Irish place that gave us the day off on March 17 and taught us to sing the great Irish ballads. I acclimated to the Irish rather well. They were much like Ukrainians. Songs were sung in public spontaneously and they were always ready to toast one another and were an outwardly friendly group.

Irish families weren't the only ones at St. Pat's. The school was filled with many Italians, Poles and Germans and they had huge families. Many had a half dozen or more kids. Even with more than four hundred students at St. Pat's, I knew which kid was in what grade and whose family she or he was in. I picked up on all the genealogy through my socializing on the playground. During our six-and-a-half hour day we had three recesses, which included eating a hurried bag lunch from home so we could spend as much time outdoors as possible. For more than an hour every day we devoted our time to games we needed to invent because no ball was allowed on the playground. Also, there was no playground equipment, no chalk for hopscotch, just asphalt and our overactive imaginations.

Supervision on the playground was minimal, maybe one or two teachers hanging around, but I don't ever remember seeing a nun outdoors. Sitting up in her third-floor window, however, was the school librarian, Sister Mary Benedict, eyes peeled on all four hundred children, watching like a hawk.

Sister Mary Benedict was a scary one. She wore the long black and white habit familiar to all nuns before Vatican II, but even after the Vatican changes she maintained her authority in full black, with only a bit of white wimple around her face. Wearing the old habit meant to all of us she was probably eighty-five years old. The only body parts visible on Sister Mary Benedict in the full habit were her face and hands. A kid could get nightmares from seeing that face of hers. It was always a furious shade of red. No one and I mean *no one* ever attempted to cross her or even hold a conversation with her. Passing her in the hallway was a dare to see if you didn't get yelled at, and if you did receive a reprimand, you could tell a good story about what blew her top. She was always looking for trouble, and if it wasn't there, she would invent it.

One day my youngest brother was running alongside the wall of her window and she yelled out to him.

"*You!* Young man! What are you doing!?"

Since he was the only person in her view, he knew she was addressing him. He didn't know what to do. He was always well behaved. He had never been in trouble before, not at home, not at school. He looked up and again she bellowed.

"*I asked*, young man, what are you doing!?"

He looked around. Checking to see what might be wrong, he couldn't find anything. He finally assembled all the courage he had and spoke very softly.

"I don't know what you mean, Sister." *Gulp.*

Her face became even redder as she fumed with rage.

"*Don't* talk back to me like that! You know what you were doing!"

The poor little guy was clueless. Again, he attempted to reason with her, trying not to imagine what kind of persecution awaited him in the third-floor torture chamber everyone was convinced she possessed.

"I...I...was...just running...Sister..." She glowered at him and gritted her teeth.

"That's right, young man, you were *running*! Now sit down over on that wall until recess is over!"

Imagine that. Running on a playground.

There was a reason word got around from the instant you were a student at St. Pat's that Sister Mary Benedict's nickname was Bulldog. Her bark would petrify any young bully on the playground. However, by the time kids left St. Pat's they figured out there was no torture equipment, no bite in her. Her threats to send anyone to the principal's office didn't faze the older students. The principal was fully aware of Sister Mary Benedict's temperament. Bulldog was simply an angry puppy.

Outside of Sister Mary Benedict, I found the nuns with whom I had contact to be congenial, and yes, they did smile and laugh often. I had a full habit nun as a teacher only once. Sister Francine too, looked eighty-five years old. I was in fifth grade and by that age kids tried messing with teachers' heads.

Sister Francine was very orderly. When I say orderly, I mean assignments needed to be handed from back to front; when you received the pile from behind you were to put your assignment on top of the pile and then move it forward. Sister Francine then started from the right side of the room, picked up the assignments, made her way left, and put each pile on the front desks on top of the pile in her hands. She would grade them, turn them over, and when handing them back they could be returned in order. Everyone needed to be in their desks with their hands folded anytime the bell rang. The top of her desk had every folder, notebook, pencil and pen in its proper place.

Looking back, I marvel at her efficiency, but when you're ten years old, you'll do anything to disrupt it just because your hormones tell you to act stupid. We would "accidentally" bump into her neat pile of assignments on her desk, sending papers flying, and she would scramble quickly to put them back in the order she wanted them. This would usually take five or ten minutes out of our lesson time, which was the whole point of our mischief. When she left the room, someone always went to her desk and rearranged it, finding great pleasure in hiding the red pen with which she corrected assignments. The pen usually ended up in a lower drawer, *way in the back*, and she'd search for it like the one lost sheep out of the one hundred. She never lost her cool, however. I think at eighty-five she probably thought it was simply her old age that made her scatter her desk items in odd places.

Sister Francine was very obedient to the Catholic Church. We had gone through the catechism for First Communion and Confirmation in earlier grades, yet we reviewed everything from the Ten Commandments to the categories of sin with her. A mortal sin was something like murder or not being Christian, which would send you to hell. A venial sin was perhaps lying and could be absolved by Confession or spending time in purgatory. We were told that Catholics went to heaven and Jews went to hell.

By fifth grade I was beginning to see the world outside of black and white rules. My big question was, where did my Protestant friends end up? I didn't want to go to a place where some of my closest friends wouldn't be partying with me!

I had also just finished reading *The Diary of Anne Frank* and the whole Jews-going-to-hell thing was really bothering me. My parents had lived right in the middle of World War II in Europe, had witnessed Jews being persecuted, had seen them in the concentration camps and were both put into forced labor by the Nazis. I had heard about the atrocities of Stalin and Hitler when my parents would sit around the table with other Ukrainians and talk about their own experiences when they thought we kids weren't listening.

One day I felt in my gut I needed to talk to Sister Francine. I asked if I could be excused from recess to have a word with her. I'm sure I had a grave look on my face, because she was willing to put her organized day aside to hear me out. The kids left and we were alone.

"What would you like to talk about, Talia?"

This wasn't easy for me, because we were always taught to respect the sisters and the Catholic Church's teachings.

"I'd like to talk to you about something that's been bothering me about our religion." I could feel the heat rise to my face and every instinct told me to run.

Something very strong held me back to stay in the room.

"Sister...we've been taught that as Catholics if we don't commit a mortal sin we will go to heaven."

"Yes, that's right."

"Well Sister, I've...I've been reading *The Diary of Anne Frank*. Have you heard of that book?"

Sister Francine stalled a bit and said, "Yes, I have."

Tears began welling up. "Well, Sister, you see...it's very hard for me..." I could feel a melt-down coming on.

"Go on, Talia."

"You see...my parents were living in Germany when the Jews were in the concentration camps. And well...they saw..." And then I couldn't hold my tears any longer. "Oh, Sister, how could God send those poor people to hell when they went through such horrible things? I don't understand!" I broke down in uncontrollable sobs while Sister Francine went silent.

Then something happened that I'd never experienced from a nun. Sister Francine took me in her arms and held me against her while I cried. I don't know if it was from compassion, or possibly she didn't want me to see her face. When my tears began to subside, she spoke so quietly, I could barely hear her.

"Don't cry, Talia, God will take good care of the Jews."

I wasn't sure if she was saying those words just to comfort me or whether she truly believed that heaven was a place for everyone. All I know is her words made such a difference in my perception of God. Taking care of people, comforting them made me see that God was more maternal than the Church's view of "God the Father." I no longer felt she or he was filled with wrath because people believe differently from other people; God became someone who loved everyone.

The recess bell was about to ring, and Sister Francine gently pulled away from me. She offered me tissues that were neatly placed on her desk. As I blew my nose and blotted my eyes, she asked, "Are you all right? Is there anything else?"

Feeling like I was on a roll with honest questions, I said, "Yes, Sister, there is. In teaching the Ten Commandments nobody has ever quite explained to me the meaning of adultery."

Sister Francine assumed her organized and distinguished role and said curtly, "You'll learn about that in eighth grade," as the rest of the class ran in to sit in their desks before the bell rang.

⌘※

One of the first things the kids noticed at St. Pat's was that my brothers and I didn't go to church there on Sundays. Their first thoughts were, "Wow, are you lucky! Your parents don't make you go to church!" Difficult as it was to dispel the myth that our parents were heathens, all three of us had the exact same discussion with our respective classmates. It went something like this:

"We go to a different kind of Catholic church. It's St. Stephen's Ukrainian Greek Catholic Church."

"So," they'd ask, "is it Ukrainian or Greek?" Fair question.

"The service is in Ukrainian, but the denomination is Greek Catholic where St. Pat's is Roman Catholic."

"So what's Ukrainian?" Another fair question.

"Ukrainians are a group of people, just like the Chinese, or Irish, or Italians or the French, who have their own country and language, but Ukraine has been taken over by the Soviet Union."

"Oh, so you're Russian."

"No, I'm Ukrainian…"

"…but you said Ukrainians were part of Russia…"

"…I said the Ukrainians were now part of the Soviet Union…"

"…but that's Russia."

Breathe, Talia, breathe…

"Let...me...explain. The Soviet Union is *not* a country. It has about a dozen countries in it that belong to the Soviet Union. Russia and Ukraine are two of them."

"So...you're a Commie?"

So...you want me to knock your teeth out?

"No...my parents left because they *didn't* want to live under Communism."

"Oh. Okay then. So, what's the difference between Greek Catholic and Normal Catholic?"

Normal Catholic?

Sigh. "The difference is it has a different liturgy..."

"...what's a liturgy?"

"It's the words you say during the service, that are a lot like the Orthodox Church..."

"...what's Orthodox...?"

"...but probably the biggest difference is that in the Greek Catholic Church, if they're ordained in Europe, priests can be married and have kids."

Pause.

"Wait a minute; you're telling me that your priests get married..."

"...yep..."

"....and you know ...have sex...and have kids?"

"Yep."

An even longer pause.

"Then you're not REALLY Catholic."

Why even try?

My brothers told me this would happen and it was just easier to say we belong to a different Catholic Church and St. Pat's was the closest Catholic school to our house. The funny thing is, I'll explain to people today what the Greek Catholic Church is about, and people will still say I was raised Orthodox.

Or that I'm Greek.

Whatever. To-may-to, to-mah-to.

We're Not Going to Talk About It

The room was enormous. I had been in it before, but I couldn't remember why. At one end of the room was a stage. *Yes, I remember*. I had watched people perform Ukrainian folk dances and songs. It seemed so long ago, when actually it was only a couple of months. Two months is a long time for a three-year-old.

My mom whispered gently in my ear.

"It's time for you to go on stage. Remember we talked about this and what song you're going to sing?"

Of course I did. I had been singing from the time I could speak. My mom took my hand and helped me walk up the steep stairs to the stage, and then walked over to the side to make sure I could see her. From the stage I couldn't see anyone in front of me. The lights were so bright, yet not blinding. Accapella, I sang a story about a lost girl looking to find her way home. It was in Ukrainian and it was simple enough that I understood the words. The performance took less than a minute. Then came the applause. I looked at my mom in the wings, who demonstrated a small curtsey and I imitated her. The applause was even louder, along with some laughter. I looked at the bright lights.

This is what heaven must be like.

I always loved being on stage and it didn't matter what I did: singing, acting, dancing, it was all a wonderful dream world for me. In Mrs. Lucyk's plays in Ukrainian school I was consistently given the female lead due to my ability to convey emotion with authority to an audience of people whose freedom and independence had come at the price of having to leave their homeland. Mrs. Lucyk knew I would give it my all. It was not rare for me to leave people in tears, performing what she'd written about the plight of courageous Ukrainian children somehow becoming the heroes at the end of a play and winning against the Great Oppressor, Josef Stalin.

As much as everyone else despised Mrs. Lucyk's constant rehearsals, I was in my element. About once a summer I would find a friend who would begrudgingly cooperate with my need to create skits and we'd put on shows in each other's backyards. Playing someone else gave me the liberty to have a life outside of myself, to do and to say things that were contradictory to what was expected of me.

As I progressed from kindergarten through my early elementary years I watched how my mom handled people with different aspects of her personality to help her connect with the world as well as get what she wanted out of it. She was a great actor and I adopted that characteristic. My dad, on the other hand, was more subtle in his behavior. He had a quietness about him that didn't waver a whole lot.

In the fall of fourth grade I was eight years old and my mom was scheduled to go into the hospital. I remembered one other such occasion while I was still quite young when she had a hysterectomy. She came out of it just fine and I was told "she can't have babies anymore." She bounced back with her usual life spirit. This time she was going in for some tests. It didn't sound dire and I had no reason to believe things would turn out badly. She didn't look sick or feel sick.

About two days into my mom's hospital stay my dad sat the three of us down and said she had breast cancer and her right breast would be removed. That was as much as he knew and for weeks afterward Mom would need to be taken to the hospital daily for radiation treatments.

Every day Dad would stop by the hospital after work to see her. He would then come home and do something I hadn't seen him do in a long time – he'd light up a cigarette and look worried. I was confused. The only knowledge I had of cancer was that if you smoked you would get lung cancer, so why was my dad smoking and what did this mean for my mom? Lung cancer in the late 1960s was more or less a death sentence.

Our class at school had just had a discussion of the dangers of smoking and lung cancer.

One day while I was walking to school a boy from my class caught up with me and we walked the rest of the way together. He noticed I wasn't quite myself. I told him my mom had been diagnosed with cancer.

"Uh oh, that's what happens when you smoke," he remarked.

I didn't know how to explain the difference between lung and breast cancer, and I certainly wasn't going to say *breast* in front of him. I felt shame for my mom, that she might have done something to have gotten this awful disease. I decided I wouldn't mention it to anyone else to spare myself any more grief.

When Mom came back home from her hospital stay she was a different woman. Usually so full of life, she was weak and sad. I had never seen her so fragile before. The three of us kids had already gotten into a household routine of cooking, cleaning up from our meals, dusting and vacuuming and we were able to ease her load. A woman from church came by once a week to do laundry. At age eight I was handling household responsibilities on a scheduled basis without having to be reminded and I began to cook simple things for the family. I did my best not to appear burdened by the role reversal. I wanted so badly to make Mom feel better and to show that I cared.

One day she took the task of watering the house plants and I could see the weariness in her eyes.

"Mom, I'm so sorry you have cancer," I told her sympathetically. Her response was not what I expected.

"We're not going to talk about it." She continued watering the plants while I stood watching her, confused by her remark.

Okay. No talking.

Another wave of shame swept over me. Apparently I'd said something wrong to her and I didn't mean to. Why didn't she want to talk? We talked about everything together, or so I thought. In one short sentence she'd made it apparent her cancer was not to be discussed.

Every week at church Father Dorosh would offer up special prayers of healing for my mom and called her on a regular basis. Each service

I would feel this churning in my stomach that kept saying to me, *we're not going to talk about it.* Week after week the petition of prayers for her health made me feel worse. Then one week they stopped. She had a clean bill of health from her doctor. We felt some relief. Despite the fact that the operation had left her disfigured and scarred, she was grateful to have come through the abominable journey.

The following fall she noticed an ache in her thigh and a second hospital stay indicated Mom had bone cancer.

She went through another series of radiation. Father Dorosh once again began the petition of prayers and the churning in my gut kept getting worse. People at church and the neighborhood were again helpful with laundry and cooking for the family, but what I needed was some clarification on what exactly was happening to my mother. No one would even mention the word cancer or ask me if I needed anything, as if avoiding the subject of her illness would somehow make it seem as if it didn't exist. Keep it under wraps, I said to myself.

We're not going to talk about it.

For a few years things appeared to be normal as my mom was put on some medications to keep her cancer dormant, but she never felt entirely well. She kept up the appearance of good health and there were no more prayer petitions, no hospital stays. However, by the time I was thirteen my mom was back in the hospital. This time she would go on a regular basis for chemotherapy. It was a new procedure in treating cancer and there had been some success. I thought radiation treatments in the past were hard on her, but the chemotherapy was a living hell with the visible nausea and vomiting. By this time Father Dorosh, who'd been such a rock in her life, was too frail to stay active in parish ministry and retired out of state. It was such a loss for my mom; the only clergyman I ever felt was truly a part of my life was leaving us at the worst possible time.

Our new priest had already been serving the Ukrainian Catholic Church in Minneapolis. He was assigned to serve St. Stephen's for worship on Saturday nights. I never saw him smile. He didn't make the effort Father Dorosh did to get to know the people of the congregation.

As far as I knew, he never phoned Mom or visited her in the hospital. I felt his petition of prayers for her was just a formality, part of his religious duty. Once again, I felt an ugly churning in the gut.

I wanted to scream at him, *"Just SHUT UP! You don't know ANYTHING about my mom!"*

The prayers my mother taught me to say morning and nighttime stopped. This God we were praying to was certainly not a God with whom I wanted any relationship.

Through the process of my mom's decline I picked up responsibilities at school that would keep me away from the house. Student Council president, leading roles in the school plays, vocal groups, trying my hardest to be Number One at anything and everything. If I couldn't make my mom better, at least I could have control over success in my own life.

And during the entire time my mantra kept pounding in my head: *We're not going to talk about it.*

As the cancer progressed it metastasized to her brain. She was experiencing memory loss. One moment she'd be completely coherent, the next she couldn't remember names, activities or that she even had cancer. I could see her literally losing her mind. As I was now an adolescent, dealing with enough of the drama that goes on during those years, keeping up a façade of composure became harder and harder. I started becoming detached from people. I neglected kids who were my friends because I couldn't handle their petty, juvenile issues. When I wasn't at school I'd spend my evenings holed up in my room, reading from books I had read dozens of times to immerse myself into someone else's world that was infinitely better than my own.

Towards the end of ninth grade in junior high, I began participating in risky behaviors. I would smoke, irregularly, but just enough to calm my nerves. It was easy to drink as my dad never governed his beer stash, and a friend's sister had adult connections to buy us cheap bottles of wine. I even dared to go into the teacher's lounge one day at school while they were having a meeting elsewhere and smoked from a teacher's pack of cigarettes. Luckily, there was no chance of me getting pregnant because I never allowed anyone to get close enough to me, physically or emotionally.

I was a mess.

One day, a group of us were walking home from school and an acquaintance of mine was up front with me.

"I don't know what's wrong with you. You've become so stuck-up it makes me feel you don't want to hang out with me anymore."

That did it. I snapped. Seething with anger and frustration, I looked him square in the eye.

"You're right! You're an idiot. I *don't* want to hang out with you!"

Nobody said anything for a short time; people simply stared at me, shocked that I would use such harsh language, as it wasn't in my nature to do so.

Even my best friend Caroline looked at me and said, "You know, that was a lousy thing to say."

"I don't care!" I screamed and sprinted away, back to my home, back to the place where even the *smell* of death was in the air. Word got around about my behavior and I was admonished by several people for my insensitivity. Even still, nobody at school knew death was living under my roof.

We're not going to talk about it.

By the following fall I was in high school and it was easy just to be a face in the crowd. I was relieved for it. It was evident without anyone saying so that my mother had very little time left. During the petitions of prayer for her I would rehearse lines from the play I was in. I did my best to keep up a sense of equanimity in school and somehow managed to have my very first date with a boy for a school dance. Mom was so weak she couldn't make it downstairs to meet him. She cried to have missed out on this important rite of passage as I left with him, despondent. I was a wet blanket the whole evening. I was losing my grip as an actor.

A few weeks before my fifteenth birthday my dad knocked on my bedroom door and I invited him in. He had an expression on his face that was unreadable. I wasn't sure if he was mad at me for something (smoking) or just casually checking up on me, so I was a bit nervous. Suddenly his quiet charm showed through his eyes and he looked me over for a bit longer than usual. The long silence was uneasy so I was about to ask him what was up. He pulled his wallet out of his pocket. He sifted through the many bills and drew out a significant amount of money.

"With everything going on with Mama, I don't know if I'll have time to get presents for your birthday or Christmas. I want you to take this money and buy yourself something very grown up and sophisticated. Get some nice high-heeled shoes and a coat to go with an outfit." He walked out before I even had a chance to thank him.

The very next day I hopped onto a bus after school and went to the juniors section of the finest department store downtown and found a sleek, navy blue sweater dress, matching hose, a smashing winter coat and the highest-heeled shoes I could wear and still walk in. I tried everything on in the dressing room. I noticed that I was becoming curvaceous and for the first time I saw myself as a young woman. I was elated! I hadn't felt this good in a long time. I swung back and forth to see myself in the three-way mirror and in an instant reality dawned on me. I stopped moving and stared at myself for what seemed an eternity. A blank, pale face reflected back at me.

I am buying my funeral outfit.

My dad couldn't come out and say it, but somehow he knew I'd be smart enough to figure it out. I was to become the woman of the house and I needed to look the part.

A few days later my mom was in such pain she needed to go back to the hospital for pain management. The very last time my brothers and I saw her alive her face was a shade of green, the fluid in the catheter bag a rusty brown. The only communication was through her eyes, a look of pleading for someone to take away the misery mixed with the irrefutable fact that she would never see her children again.

I left, absolutely dazed.

The next day the hospital called us. She wasn't going to make it more than twenty-four hours. My dad told us to stay home, to spare us any more pain. When he came home from the hospital, he dropped the suitcase and cried.

She had died alone.

I called Caroline to tell her the news. She'd had no idea how bad things had gotten.

No one did.

❈❈

During the visitation I was dressed to the nines, gracious, forever the actor, seizing onto the role as hostess. I made small talk with ease.

We're not going to talk about it.

People were amazed at my composure. At the funeral, while everyone else chanted and wept, I sat feeling completely alone with no emotion in my body and soul. The priest offered petitions of prayer for the departed soul of Anna Makovets'ka, yet never once came up to me to offer his condolences. I looked at him and suddenly felt rage.

Your prayers are goddamn worthless.

Four months later, my dad went to the doctor because of something tickling his throat. The doctor wanted him to go into the hospital for some tests.

They removed a tumor. It was malignant.

I was fifteen years old.

I had spent six years watching my mom die a slow, agonizing death and now my dad had cancer.

I took my place at center stage. The bright lights shined on me and I carried on without seeing what or who was in front of me. No one at school, not even Caroline, knew about my dad.

We're not going to talk about it.

Everything going on at home was put into a very tight compartment to slowly and gradually fester within me. I had my mother's legacy to live up to.

I was taught to be an actor by the very best.

Things Not to Say When Someone Loses a Loved One

"**G**od won't give you more than you can handle."
Then this isn't really happening.

"Your (loved one) wouldn't want you to cry."
Let me see someone you love die and watch you not cry.

At the casket: "Doesn't your (loved one) look good?"
Really? I mean, REALLY?

"I feel so bad; how will you ever get by without your (loved one)?"
I don't know; you tell me.

"If there's anything I can do..."
Don't say it unless you call me and follow up.

"We all have to die sometime."
I can make that happen for you.

"I know how you feel."
You think you do, but you really don't.

"It's all a part of God's plan."

So God told you his plan; please enlighten me.

"God needed another angel in heaven."

Omygod, did you really say that? I'm in the worst emotional grief I have ever experienced and you're telling me God needed my (loved one) more than I do? Are you fucking insane?!

"I'm sorry for your loss."

I am too. Thank you.

College Prep

Life moved forward for me, my brothers and my dad. He was fortunate that his malignant tumor was completely removed during the biopsy and he received cobalt radiation every day after work for several weeks. He had some long term side effects from the radiation to his salivary glands and vocal cords, but for all intents and purposes his life was back to normal within a year. By the time I was a senior in high school, we all felt we could breathe a deep sigh of relief.

Out of the experience, something serendipitous happened. Since we had Saturday night church, Sunday mornings were spent with my dad at the kitchen table drinking coffee and talking. Between jobs and school and my mom's and dad's cancer there had hardly been any time for me and my brothers to bond closely with either parent. We always observed Sundays as the day you did absolutely no work inside or outside the house. So by the end of my high school days my relationship with my dad finally grew from child-parent to adult-adult. He became my friend, and over coffee we would talk about my dreams and goals, how after having cancer he felt less stressed and was not so quick to get angry about insignificant things.

The time had come for me to start thinking about furthering my education beyond high school. Higher education – whether it was college, trade school or the military – was something Ukrainian kids had no option to say "no" to. Why in the world would our parents have travelled so far if their kids weren't going to be forced to follow the American Dream?

Just about every kid growing up at St. Stephen's took part in higher education in the Twin Cities area and continued to live at home. I would have received a good education at many of the local colleges, but I had an itch to get out of town and live on a campus. My dad was dubious of the prospect of letting me go. I would be starting college at age seventeen and without anyone keeping an eye on me, who knew what I would get myself into? I didn't bother telling him the worst of my behaviors had happened in junior high and that I now had all of my rebellion out of my system.

When I brought up the idea of visiting a Lutheran college specializing in music out of town he didn't say anything. I drove there with a friend and liked the place. He could see I was committed to getting accepted to this school. I filled out all the paperwork for entrance and financial aid, only needing him to sign the papers. He complied and watched as my plans were unfolding.

I was required to send in a pastor's recommendation and if I wasn't involved in any church, a recommendation from someone who could attest to my character. Unfortunately the same grim-faced priest who performed my mother's funeral was the person I had to deal with. He noticed the recommendation was not for a Catholic college and I received an insolent sneer. I explained to him that I wanted to attend that particular school for their music program. The Monsignor snatched the form from me, muttered under his breath and gave me a begrudging look. I had made it as easy as possible for him, filling in basic information and even calling him two weeks before the due date. As we spoke on the phone he growled and said he had already mailed it. All my paperwork was sent way ahead of time and the admissions department was satisfied with my testing scores and grade point average.

A month later, I received a letter stating that I would be put on a waiting list because my admission paperwork was incomplete as it was lacking a pastor's recommendation.

What the hell...?

I showed the letter to my dad as he had been right there with me when I'd called the priest. Stunned, I asked my dad's advice. He told me by all means, get another character reference and he'd talk with the Monsignor.

After church the next Saturday evening he told my brothers and me to take the car home as he was going to discuss the recommendation with the priest and he would walk the short distance back. He was gone much longer than I had expected. When he arrived home his face was livid. He told me about his meeting. The priest had lied to me and never sent in the recommendation. The Monsignor said he "must have just forgotten." He began to apologize but my dad didn't buy it.

My guess was there was more to that conversation than my dad wished to admit.

Memories of my mom's funeral came back to me. The priest didn't show me any care or concern when she died and in my eyes he didn't give a rip about me now, either. After experiencing the integrity of Father Dorosh, the wonderful love he showed each and every person in that congregation, I couldn't fathom how I could be lied to by a clergyman.

"Dad, how could a priest, someone we're supposed to go to for consolation and advice, do something to purposely sabotage my education?

He hesitated awhile to think, then gave me a straight look and said, "Talia, we don't really know what his intentions were. He could have forgotten or he could have done it on purpose. If his intention was to not send it in, I hate to say this, but this won't be the first time someone will betray you."

Welcome to the real world, Talia.

I made plans to attend the University of Minnesota for my freshman year and hoped I could transfer afterward. Three weeks before the fall semester was to begin I received a call from the college I wanted to attend. They had an opening. I turned to Dad, telling him they wanted me at orientation in less than a month.

He smiled and said, "You go right ahead and say yes."

When I was finished with the phone call I gave him a big hug and I ran up to my bedroom to start making lists of what I needed for my move. He followed me upstairs and asked me to sit down.

"I want you to remember what happened with the Monsignor. Even if he tried to interfere with your plans you still managed to get into the college of your choice this fall. Life doesn't always happen this way. So I hope when you attend this school you will be as respectful to their religion as hopefully they will be to yours. What people believe is *holy* to them, and even if you don't agree with their faith, respect their freedom to call it their own."

How did my dad get so smart?

I didn't want to burst his bubble and tell him I had no interest in religion, especially after watching my mom suffer so badly and the Monsignor acting so callous during the funeral. His shenanigans about my recommendation only furthered my distrust in anything having to do with the Church.

Nevertheless, I got the gist of what he was trying to convey to me. My dad had seen a lot in his life. He'd witnessed families torn apart because of religious differences, heard of the millions of people who starved and died under Stalin because they were Ukrainians and had set eyes on the skeletal figures of the Jews in the concentration camps. I was just beginning to realize what he and my mom had endured and I saw my parents, for the very first time, as courageous and more importantly, forgiving.

All of a sudden I was sad I was going to leave and I told my dad as much. He laughed.

"Believe me," he said, "you won't have much time to miss me. Besides, you'll only be a short distance away. I crossed the world when I left my family."

He was about to walk away when he turned around and gave me a long stare. He had a stern look about him and gave a few last words of advice to me.

"Be careful when you leave and go live on your own. You *know* what I mean."

I started to giggle.

I knew he was talking about sex, a subject we had never discussed and he wasn't all that comfortable making conversation on the topic.

I fell back on my bed, snickering at him. He tried to get serious but failed.

"You *know* what I mean!" he kept saying, pointing his finger at me but I couldn't stop laughing. "I don't want your studies going to waste with you living away from home and you all of a sudden becoming pr.... you *know* what I mean!"

He tried his best to remain stern and was relentless to keep from breaking his strict demeanor. By this time I was doubled over and howling hysterically. My poor dad. He was doing his best to have "the talk" with me and I was being a brat. He gave me one last look, shook his head, smirked, and left the room before he could no longer contain his own laughter.

The next Saturday he went into the Monsignor's office and told him I was accepted at the Lutheran college. Without waiting for a response he turned around, whistled his way out the door and met me with his famous shit-eating grin. He swaggered out of the church and I swaggered along with him.

Culture Shock

Moving day for college came, and with it, the nervousness anyone would have when life makes a significant change. I was only an hour's drive from home, yet I felt a thousand miles away. Back in those days, the only way to communicate was by land line or snail mail.

The college I attended was founded by a group of Norwegian Lutherans back in the late nineteenth century. As I looked around the campus of students unloading their belongings, I was submerged in a sea of blondes and redheads. Many students were second, third, even fourth generation of freshmen entering this academic institution. I felt completely out of place as a Ukrainian Greek Catholic, knowing very little about Scandinavian Lutheran tradition.

One friend I made on campus felt the way I did, and I would say, even more so. That friend was my roommate. She came from a prestigious background, knowing first-hand people from the civil rights movement of the 1960s, was raised as a single child from upper-middle class parents in Chicago, and was African-American. The college couldn't have picked two people to room together who came from more opposite upbringings even if they tried. We did find we had something in common – a boyfriend back home, or as it was defined in college, an "HTH" – Home Town Honey. Nothing will get two girls talking more quickly than pouting together about having to leave a person behind that, for heaven's sakes, we'd have surely eventually married if school hadn't separated us. By the end of freshman year, ninety-nine percent of those with an HTH had either dumped their boyfriends or became the dumpees.

Every freshman "corridor" housed two juniors to help the newbies become acquainted to the campus. After dinner our first evening, all twenty of us on the corridor packed ourselves into one dorm room and got the lowdown of the facilities in the building. Despite being on a meal plan, we had a kitchen in the dorm which we could use at any time if we wanted to cook or bake something ourselves.

One of the Scandinavians on my corridor (I'm assuming she was, since she was part of the blonde contingency), asked the juniors whether or not the kitchen had a lefse griddle.

My roommate was sitting next to me. She looked at me and muttered under her breath, "What the hell is a lefse griddle?"

I was as puzzled as her. "I have no clue, but something tells me we'll eventually find out."

We did. Later on in December we were graced with a traditional Norwegian Christmas meal. It was complete with lutefisk – cod soaked in lye – rice pudding with lingonberries, and of course, lefse – a Scandinavian tortilla made out of potatoes. Edible enough, except for the lutefisk. After my first bite of this rather smelly "delicacy" I graciously declined it subsequent years to allow those who had built up cast-iron stomachs to a second helping.

My roommate and I learned a lot from each other. Simply being around her as well as others from the African-American community, I became more understanding of the prejudice and discrimination toward her and her heritage. Although the intolerance I received from people who enjoyed calling me a Communist was uncomfortable, I discovered the degree of bigotry my roommate and other African-Americans faced was despicable.

By sophomore year I had established a group of friends who stayed with me all through graduation. I'd had the same people in the same music classes, and among the other musicians I was able to find some wonderful companions. Much of my time was spent in the cafeteria, drinking copious amounts of coffee and using mealtime as an excuse to gab away the hours.

My most favorite spot by far was the theatre building. Anyone who has been involved in theatre knows you will never find the kind of friendships you make with theatre people in any other environment. We're all bizarre. Weird, freaky lifestyles, peculiar forms of dress, walking around speaking in various dialects, spending the night in the building without a custodian telling you to leave, all of it was good.

For some reason, I became one of the few people some in the theatre department were willing to "come out" to and talk about their homosexuality, and I kept their information private. I saw how difficult it was for them to want to express their true selves, yet the culture of the time made the subject closeted and shameful. The prejudice was as prevalent as it was for African-Americans. Word got around and soon students from the music department were willing to share their feelings with me. I asked a gay friend of mine why it seemed as if I had more gay friends than any other woman on campus. His reply was people felt safe around me. I didn't realize it at the time, but my dad's words about respecting other people's religion transferred to respecting people's sexual orientation as well as their race.

Between the music and theatre buildings, I came to love so many. I found kindred spirits, sometimes through the oddest circumstances because I was willing to step outside my comfort zone and to think out-of-the-box to create my own artistic opportunities. I learned to accept myself as a revolutionary person and was encouraged by others to be radical. I broke away from the norms of the classical music we were taught and cultivated my own personal, imaginative style in the arts. It was a wonderful springboard for my entrance into adult life.

Life was good. Life couldn't have been any better.

It was at that point life decided to turn around and bite me in the ass.

DSM-IV

Cast of Characters in Order of Appearance

TALIA (age 19)

TALIA (age 32)

FIRST DOCTOR

TALIA'S FATHER

SECOND DOCTOR

TALIA (age 37)

IRINA (Talia's Daughter, age 11)

JODY (Irina's friend)

CORRINE (Jody's mother)

BECKY (Talia's friend)

MONIQUE (Talia's friend)

PSYCHIATRIST

TALIA (age 19)

In her college chapel building, Talia is in rehearsal on a Saturday for the next day's worship service. The rehearsal ends and everyone leaves except for her. She is feeling out of sorts. She looks around the chapel, sees the stain-glassed windows and notices the colors becoming more pronounced. The stain-glassed windows meld into one color. She becomes lightheaded to the point where she cannot stand. Her heartbeat is racing. She feels dizzy and sits in a pew with her head between her knees in an attempt to avoid fainting. She takes deep breaths and her heartbeat slowly returns to normal. She looks at the stained glass and the colors are still melded to-gether. She continues to take deep breaths and gradually the stained-glass windows return to their normal colors. She decides to stand up and feels able to walk. She is confused by what has happened.

Talia walks to the cafeteria, hoping she will feel better after she eats. She looks up at the menu and above it sees the date. November 3. It is her mother's birthday.

Over the next month Talia experiences other peculiarities. Objects become sharpened in color and their forms have light-colored edging. She feels a constant unease. Nothing hurts, but she has never felt worse in her life. She is prone to crying and becomes anxious easily. She panics when singing in public. She cannot control her singing voice or her anxiety. The anxiety comes and goes several times a day. She has a hard time falling asleep at night.

Talia notices that crowds annoy her. It is difficult to find places to be alone, which causes more anxiety. One evening she walks into her dorm room and twenty people are packed in it for a surprise birthday party for her. The din of the crowd is overwhelming. When the guests have left she gives her roommate a hug for being so gracious. She hopes her roommate doesn't feel her shaking.

Talia is concerned that she cannot handle the stress of her finals. She is adamant about finishing the semester and studies for finals when she is not panic-stricken. She now has difficulty staying asleep. She is so exhausted that she often sees herself going through motions without any thought to what she is doing.

Talia finishes her finals and travels home. There she sleeps twelve hours or more each day throughout her winter break. By January she feels her anxiety slowly abating. She assumes her physical and emotional state over the previous month and a half was due to exhaustion.

TALIA (age 32)

Talia has developed a chest cold. She feels as if a brick is sitting on her lungs. She has a chronic cough. She continues working her job yet day by day her stamina diminishes. After three weeks of her illness she is so weak she must sit after walking up a flight of stairs. She is exhausted; however, when falling asleep she wakes up with a jolt. Each time it occurs, she feels more adrenaline entering her system. She becomes so ill she cannot go to her job and calls her physician for an appointment. She sees him the next day.

FIRST DOCTOR

Tell me what's been going on.

Talia explains her symptoms to the doctor. He sends her to the imaging center and she receives a chest x-ray. She returns to the waiting room and a nurse calls her into the doctor's examining room.

FIRST DOCTOR

Your chest x-rays show your lungs are clear. The heavy weight you feel is more than likely pleurisy which is an inflammation of the lung tissue. It's not life threatening. It has probably been caused by the amount of coughing you've been doing. You can ease the weight by putting a heating pad on your chest.

TALIA

But what about my exhaustion? Why am I waking up with jolts and not sleeping?

FIRST DOCTOR

Let me prescribe an anti-depressant we use for a sleeping aid. Because it isn't a tranquilizer, it won't be habit-forming.

Talia fills the prescription. She takes one pill at bedtime and jolts out of her sleep several times. Three hours later she falls asleep and sleeps through the night.

Talia now has been ill for two months and is on short-term disability from work. She is constantly fatigued. Some nights she falls asleep right away, some nights the adrenaline jolts her awake and she cannot sleep at all. One night she is awoken by a jolt and her breathing becomes shallow. She cannot catch her breath. She tries to breathe deeply, but feels she cannot get any air in her lungs. Talia begins to panic. It is the middle of the night and she needs to get to a hospital. She calls her father and asks him to come over to her house to stay with her five-year-old daughter, Irina. Upon his arrival, she calls 911 and an ambulance picks her up. She is put on oxygen and arrives at the hospital. She is connected to various devices and with the oxygen flowing into her lungs her panic subsides. The hospital cannot find anything that would make her breathing so labored. The emergency room releases her and tells her to make an appointment with her physician as a follow- up. She calls a taxi and comes home in time to wake Irina for school. She changes her mind about her daughter attending school that day and lets her sleep. Talia's father leaves and she calls the school to say Irina will be absent. She makes an appointment with her physician later that day. She enters Irina's room and gently lies next to her. Irina stirs and Talia takes her in her arms.

Later that afternoon Talia is met by her doctor in the examining room. She explains to him what occurred during the night. He listens more closely to her lungs. She is experiencing tics on her eyelids and sees that the doctor notices them as well.

FIRST DOCTOR

How have you been sleeping?

TALIA

Not very well. Some nights not at all.

FIRST DOCTOR

Any new symptoms?

TALIA

There are times when I feel an itch under my skin. It feels as if there are spiders crawling on my insides.

FIRST DOCTOR

Keep taking the medication I prescribed last time. I'm also going to give you one prescription that is a tranquilizer to help you sleep. Take one only when you absolutely need to. (*He pauses for a moment.*) I'm also going to suggest you see a specialist in Behavioral Health.

TALIA

(*Hesitantly*)...I'm not sure I follow...

FIRST DOCTOR

A psychiatrist. I have a referral and I suggest you make an appointment.

Talia takes the new prescription and the referral from him. She feels the doctor doesn't know what he's talking about. She is experiencing sleep deprivation, twitching and exhaustion. She does not feel despondent in any way.

Talia is taking one sleeping pill almost daily; sometimes she takes two. Over the course of a month she is counting how many pills are left. When she has taken all of them she calls her doctor's office and asks to see a different physician.

SECOND DOCTOR

Please describe what's been going on.

Talia reiterates her symptoms to her.

SECOND DOCTOR

I see by your records a recommendation was made for a psychiatric analysis. Have you been evaluated by a psychiatric specialist?

TALIA

No, not yet. I just need to get some sleep and I know I'll feel better.

SECOND DOCTOR

(She hesitates) I'll write out just one more prescription for the tranquilizer you've been taking. And do make an appointment to see the psychiatrist.

Talia leaves the doctor's office. She considers calling the psychiatrist, but still feels that she is doing well emotionally. Slowly, over the course of six months, her sleep patterns return to normal. She goes back to work half-time, and within a year she is working full-time again.

TALIA (age 37)

Talia is pacing the floor in a cabin in northern Wisconsin. It is 2:00 a.m. Irina and her girlfriend Jody are asleep in a loft above Talia's room. For three months Talia has been experiencing fatigue and jolts of adrenaline again. Every object she looks at has an outline around it. When she is alone, she cries uncontrollably. She is frustrated, confused, and feels as if she is watching herself from the outside, not even within her body. Sometimes she wonders if she has died, and is observing from some dark place what is happening on earth.

Talia leaves the cabin and walks a half mile into the woods with a flashlight. She screams and finds herself rocking back and forth. She continues to do this for ten minutes. At the point when her throat becomes too sore to scream anymore she runs as fast as she can back to the cabin. She imagines demons are chasing her. She enters, exhausted, and wonders if her sense of reason has left her. She is terrified. She opens her purse and pulls out her wallet. She takes out a piece of paper and begins pacing the floor.

Talia is still carrying the recommendation to the psychiatrist that was given to her five years earlier. She has feared making an appointment because she is paranoid her ex-husband will sue for custody of Irina, despite the fact that everything has been amicable over the years. She continues pacing and finally ends up on her knees sobbing, her head lying on the bed and her arms stretched out, clinging to the bed in fear that if she lets go she will sink into a deep, frightening pit.

Suddenly, Talia feels as if she is being drawn to a new place. She is neither peaceful nor in anguish. Her emotions are dead. She hears in her mind these words: "Talk to me." Talia follows what her mind is saying.

TALIA

I feel someone is with me...who are you...? What am I supposed to talk about? *(Talia hesitates and speaks slowly)* I know who you are... *(Talia hesitates for a long while)* I don't want you in my life. *(Talia is expecting an answer but doesn't hear one.)* You said TALK TO ME, DAMMIT! Why don't YOU say anything!!?? *(Talia continues to wait for an answer.)* All right, you son-of-a-bitch...I'll talk! *(Talia holds back her thoughts for a while and then decides to speak her mind.)* You disappointed me, you know that? You *REALLY* disappointed me. I was just a kid and you made ME and my FAMILY and ESPECIALLY MY MOTHER go through a LIVING HELL! You know what? God damn yourself!! YOU...YOU who sit high and mighty and watch people go INSANE and you do absolutely nothing! NOTHING!! *(Talia collects her thoughts and continues.)* And another thing, you bastard – where the hell were you when my marriage was falling apart? I gave my heart, everything to a man, RIGHT in front of your altar and you did NOTHING to save my marriage! I HATE YOU!! I DESPISE even your name! We are told OVER and OVER and OVER that if we pray YOU have the power to change things. I've NEVER seen any help coming from your direction, you SON-OF-A-BITCH! How DARE you call yourself the God who loves us! GOD...WHY...DON'T...YOU... HELP ME...PLEASE...HELP...MEEEEEE......!

Talia again begins sobbing. She sobs uncontrollably for several minutes. Slowly her sobs become less intense and in a short time they stop completely. She feels nothing. No hurt, no joy, no emotion. She lies down on her bed. She has received an answer. She knows she will not sleep tonight. It doesn't matter to her anymore. She has made a decision. She waits until a reasonable hour of the morning. She gets out of bed and walks up the flight of stairs to the loft. She opens the door and sees Irina and Jody sleeping amongst a room full of clutter. She walks over to Irina and gently nudges her. Irina's eyes open and Talia begins to speak.

TALIA

...Honey...I'm very sorry...We need to pack up and go home. I'm very sick...I don't know what's wrong with me, but I need to go to a hospital. Please get everything packed as quickly as possible. (*Irina gives Talia a frightened look.*) Don't worry; everything will be okay. Just pack up and we'll leave for home.

Irina stares at her mother, bewildered. Talia motions to her to wake up Jody and leaves the room. Talia walks downstairs and begins packing everything she brought from home. Fifteen minutes later Irina and Jody have their suitcases packed and throw them into the trunk of the car. They help Talia finish packing, cleaning and loading up the car. As the girls sit in the back seat, Talia sits at the table in the cabin and writes out a check, a note to the owner of the cabin, and leaves the key on the table. She shuts all the doors, walks to the car and begins the two hour drive home. Halfway through she sees a rural cemetery. She feels envy for those underneath the gravestones.

When she arrives home, Talia parks the car on the street instead of the garage. She calls Jody's mother, Corinne, and explains to her that they are back from the cabin early and she needs to get to a hospital. Corinne offers to take Irina to her home, for as long as needed. Talia accepts her offer and thanks her, hangs up the phone and sits down. Irina has come downstairs from her room by herself.

IRINA

Mommy...? Are you going to be okay?

TALIA

That's why I'm going to the hospital, sweetheart. To get better.

Irina is looking at her mother, is about to speak, but hesitates. She then chooses to say what is on her mind.

IRINA

(*Very softly*) Mommy...do you feel like killing yourself?

Talia feels her heart shattering. Tears begin flowing freely. She takes Irina by the hand and sits her on her lap.

TALIA

Honey, I feel really bad. Worse than I've ever felt in my life. But I *promise* you I love you too much to hurt you by taking my life. I will NEVER, do you understand, NEVER, EVER hurt you like that. I'm going to the hospital and I'll do everything I need to do to become healthy again so I can be the best mom possible. I want you to believe me. Do you believe me? You know I wouldn't lie about something like this.

Irina remains quiet and then gently nods her head. She puts her head on Talia's shoulder and wraps her arms around her. Talia once again feels no emotion. They sit together like this for several minutes until she hears a knocking at the door. One of Talia's friends, Becky, has driven by, and has seen the car parked in front of the house and wonders why she is home early from her vacation. Talia explains her condition. Becky is a nurse and asks her for her health insurance card. Making several phone calls she finds out which hospital Talia needs to go to for mental health emergency. She also calls another friend, Monique, to come to the house to take Talia to the hospital. She hangs up. At that moment, Corinne comes in the door to pick up both the girls and bring them to her home. Talia and Irina hold each other tight for a long while, and then Talia lets go of her. Before leaving, Irina gives Talia one last concerned look and both she and Talia wonder what the future will hold for the two of them. Irina, Jody and Corinne leave the house. Momentarily, Talia is picked up by Monique and is driven to the hospital.

At the emergency room Talia is asked to fill out several pages of paperwork on family history of mental health, life-changing circumstances, symptoms and anything else that would benefit the attending psychiatrist to assess her condition. She quietly waits for someone to come in. Shortly, a man enters, introduces himself and lays a book down on the table. He sits down and reads Talia's paperwork.

PSYCHIATRIST

Tell me why you're here.

TALIA

I'm here because I feel my world is falling apart, and I can't understand why. Everything in my life is going well, my work, my relationships yet I feel like I'm going crazy.

PSYCHIATRIST

You don't understand why you're feeling so awful?

TALIA

No, I really don't.

PSYCHIATRIST

Let me read to you some of the things you wrote:
  Marital status: Divorced.
  Mother: Deceased. Died of cancer after a six-year illness at age forty-eight. Hospitalized once for depression. Received electro-convulsive treatment during hospitalization. Lived in Ukraine under Poland, then Stalin. Left her village at sixteen and was put into forced labor under Hitler. Likely sexual abuse as a child.
  Father: Living. In good health. Throat cancer in 1975 and recovered. Hospitalized once for depression. Received electro-convulsive treatment during hospitalization. Lived under Poland. Left his village at nineteen and was put into forced labor under Hitler.
  Maternal grandmother: Deceased. Likely Paranoid-Schizophrenic. Known attempts at suicide: two. Never married. Two infants deceased. Possible infanticide in the death of her two children.

Maternal grandfather: Known by mother but no information.

Paternal grandmother: Died of cancer when father was seventeen. Three children under the age of five deceased from smallpox. Treated for depression.

Paternal grandfather: Deceased. Alcoholic.

(*Psychiatrist puts down Talia's paperwork on the table.*) You have quite a family history of trauma, including trauma in your own life. And you don't understand why you feel so awful?

(*Talia says nothing.*)

Do you feel as if you are a threat to yourself or anyone else?

(*Talia shakes her head indicating no.*)

You understand that you need to be seen by a psychiatrist? On a regular basis? (*Talia nods.*) I'm going to start you on anti-depressants and an anti-anxiety prescription. I'm also giving you the name of a clinic near your home that has several psychiatrists you can choose from who will help manage your medications, or change them if necessary. I also have some recommendations for psychologists. You need to see one regularly for talk therapy. By starting on these medications do you feel comfortable going back home?

Talia nods. She notices the book the doctor brought in with him. It is entitled "Diagnostic and Statistical Manual of Mental Disorders, Fourth Edition" and points to it.

TALIA

Am I in that book?

PSYCHIATRIST

The DSM-IV? Yes, you are. I would say more than likely several times. (*He looks at Talia and sees her lip quivering.*)

TALIA

(*Holding back tears*) Doctor, am I going crazy?

PSYCHIATRIST

The fact that you're here and know you need help tells me you're not.

Talia sheds a single tear that slides onto her lip. She tastes the salt and realizes there is still life within her.

TALIA

My parents used to say they knew hell existed because they were in it and they didn't have to die to get there. My mom once told me her worst illness was her nervous breakdown. I'm having one too, aren't I?

He says nothing, but keeps looking at Talia for her to draw her own conclusion.

TALIA

Is this what hell feels like?

PSYCHIATRIST

Many I've talked to have said so.

Talia takes in a deep breath, and as she exhales she is surprisingly relieved. A peace has found her and she no longer fears what lies ahead.

PSYCHIATRIST

Have you gone to any counseling or spoken to anyone about your losses, your emotions...anything?

TALIA

Only once. Last night, briefly.

PSYCHIATRIST

What have you been doing all this time to cope with your pain?

TALIA

I've been an actor. (*Talia's eyes drain tears without sobs.*) A very good one...

Facing the Demons

We're not going to talk about it.
How deadly those words can be.

I made the appointment to the psychiatric clinic referred to me and the psychiatrist pinpointed my DSM-IV diagnoses: Chronic Depression, Anxiety, and Post-Traumatic-Stress-Disorder (PTSD).

I am certifiably mentally ill.

With the medication I was finally able to sleep, some days up to fifteen hours. My exhaustion wasn't just physical; I had been on an emotional roller coaster for thirty years.

Upon my psychiatrist's recommendation I made an appointment to see a therapist, someone with whom I could talk to on a regular basis for counseling. I called and made an appointment and the day before I was going to meet her I cancelled.

I'm doing better...my meds are working, I'm sleeping, I can pass cemeteries without wondering how serene it would be to be lying there...I don't need a therapist.

After I cancelled, I walked into Irina's room to grab her clothes to do laundry, and I went ballistic. I had asked her to clean her room and she hadn't done it.

"Son-of-a-bitch, Irina, I swear if I keep seeing all this shit cluttering up your room I'm going to torch everything you own!" I began throwing clothes, hangers, jewelry, anything I could find.

Lucky for her, she was in school.

I obviously needed therapy.

What kind of an example would I be to my daughter if all I did was take medication as a band-aid to cover the emotional wounds? I could go on in life as a walking zombie, but what would that mean for her? She needed a mother, and I knew what it felt like not to have one.

I made a second appointment and began a working relationship with a therapist named Jillian. I spent months in therapy with her. Progress was happening, but I was impatient. I wanted to get better, and I wanted it now, dammit!

"Jillian, how much longer do I need to keep up this therapy? Every time I come here, I feel I've moved forward about as slowly as a turtle. This is exhausting!"

Jillian pointed out, "I believe you're making good progress. You've spent three decades suppressing your issues; they won't go away overnight."

Another curveball...oh, joy...

Besides dealing with this illness, I've also had to deal with people who attach a stigma to it. Believe it or not, yes, there are still some who equate all mental illnesses with being crazy. That's okay. I'm used to being labeled. I am a Divorcee. I am a Single Parent. I am a "Sinner" because I ally with the Lesbian-Gay-Bisexual-Transgender (LGBT) community. I am Socially Progressive. I am Mentally Ill.

I spent most of my life as an actor, both on-stage and off. Even when a person is acting off-stage it isn't necessarily a bad thing. I can stand up straight, dress in a suit, put on my professional look and use proper language when I'm at a job interview or soliciting funds for a project.

Unfortunately, from the time my mother first had cancer when I was eight years old, I portrayed a demeanor that was upbeat and never spoke of anything that was troubling me emotionally. Through her illness, her death, my father's illness, my divorce, I kept up a pretense that I was strong and could handle those stresses all by myself. I became a perfectionist to appease myself against the circumstances I couldn't control. So besides dealing with my three DSM-IV diagnoses I also had no idea who my authentic self was. I'd acted my way through life.

A friend from high school pinpointed my personality so clearly. Fifteen years after graduation he saw me walking along a street and stopped to say hello. I invited him to come to my house, just a few blocks away.

He confessed, "You know, Talia, all of us guys wanted to date you, but we didn't know how to approach you. You were always the "mystery girl."

Mystery girl was a wonderful choice of words. So much pain inside was a secret to everyone. All my emotional baggage was stuffed so tightly it eventually had to burst.

I call all this baggage "junk." It's the kind of junk that makes me feel so crappy sometimes I don't even want to get out of bed. The kind of junk that keeps nagging that if I were just more motivated, life would be more productive and less depressing. Unfortunately, mental illness has very little to do with motivation. Sometimes I will have a PTSD episode simply by watching something on TV that parallels a painful experience I've had. Most importantly, I had to come to a realization that somehow, in some way, I needed to face up to my demons because frankly, my mental illness will never entirely go away.

On my computer desk sits a picture of my parents in the early 1950s surrounded by a group of their Ukrainian friends. My mom is smiling wide, my dad is grinning, and their friends are looking like they are having a great time. I believe on that day, at that moment, my parents were a happy young couple in their twenties. They were in America and for the most part, probably thought they left their junk behind in Eastern Europe.

My parents were sixteen and nineteen years old when they left their respective villages in 1942. Neither of them knew who the bad guys or the good guys were. Stalin was so demonic they imagined Hitler could be their savior. In a few short months they discovered they'd gone from the frying pan into the fire. Of the millions of innocent women, men and children who had perished, they and their Ukrainian, Polish and German friends were the minority that survived and ended up in the

United States to prosper with jobs, independence, and freedom to live their lives any way they chose. Many of them probably made decisions in Europe they would never have made under different circumstances. They may have even compromised their morals just to make it through one more day.

We're not going to talk about it.

We all pay a price by stuffing trauma.

My encounter with God at the cabin was a breakthrough, but it was just the tip of the iceberg. I will be on behavioral health medication for the rest of my life. Any time I try to wean myself off of my meds under my psychiatrist's watch has been a disaster. And being on medication doesn't ever take my condition away completely. I have to engage in work, hard work with Jillian on a regular basis for my mental health tune-ups.

Despite this illness, one significant thing has changed. I had to humble myself by admitting I couldn't go at it alone.

When I think I have everything all figured out, I'll have an episode of any one of the three diagnoses and my humility returns without hesitation.

It also appears because I was born with either the gift or the curse of creativity, my episodes of depression, anxiety or PSTD are likely to be more prominent. As I hear of artists like Hemingway, Van Gogh, Mozart, Schumann, Sylvia Plath, Virginia Woolf, the many musical and Hollywood celebrities of today who use drugs to cope, I wonder if they would have given up their creative gifts just to feel normal.

Many people who look as healthy as possible, who have achieved great accomplishments often bear the burden of never being able to talk about their own problems. They are put on pedestals where every move they make is being followed or scrutinized.

One pastor in the Twin Cities had a Sunday radio program. He was so inspiring he could make anyone who listened to him understand why he was a believer. I often called in to the program and had such amazing discussions with him. I know he made a difference in many people's lives, mine being one. Imagine my shock to find out that when he retired to Arizona he took his own life. Who even knew what his hell was?

I was at ground zero at the cabin. There were no choices I could make on my own anymore. I had, in a very odd way, a holy intervention. As I admitted to the doctor, I was in hell and I didn't have to die to get there. An intervention was the only way I could move forward, some strange, obscure voice that said "talk to me." Perhaps I was so far gone I may have hallucinated hearing a voice. Or perhaps I wasn't hallucinating.

One piece of advice to anyone who has put off seeing a psychiatrist: I don't suggest anyone getting to the low point I was at to all of a sudden become enlightened. There is nothing honorable in being sadistic to yourself to the point of feeling you're going crazy so you can experience a "God Moment."

I was taken down from my pompous attitude of going at it alone. I still carry the weight of arrogance just as I carry the weight of mental illness. I need constant humbling. That is part of my junk.

Along with that junk however, there is also hope. I was in hell and in a very real way I experienced resurrection.

So to myself, who tried to control everything I could, thought if I was just a little stronger I'd be fine, put on an act that life was a bowl of cherries, felt I could fix my problems on my own and I could sweep away all the pain and shove it under a doormat, I made a resolution:

Talia, I accept myself for having junk.

Meeting the Family

I hate getting up early. I hear of people boasting about how the best part of the day is just before sunrise when the birds begin their lyrical songs and the Eastern sky is shaded in pink and peach and magenta. There's a stillness in the air, not a car is in sight and open water has been untouched by anything to break its film. *UGGGHHH.* Getting up before mid-morning for me requires a strong, hot caffeinated drink and even after that it takes a good hour for the cobwebs in my head to clear.

Sundays had been for most of my life my day to sleep in and to slowly enjoy my hot, euphoric beverage. My ritual of coffee in the morning has not changed in decades. I begin by opening the bag of coffee from my freezer and taking a deep whiff, which immediately throws my endorphins into ecstasy mode. After pouring my first cup, the fresh smell aromatically wraps itself around me. I'm willing to miss sunrises with pleasure.

After I became a single parent so many years ago, I decided my skepticism about churches was my own issue. My three-year-old daughter was beginning to ask questions about God, as her day-care provider had the children say grace before lunch and they sang songs about Jesus. I took Irina to a neighborhood Presbyterian Church I had once attended with a high school friend and when my daughter asked to go back, I figured if your kid wants to go to church, it might not be a bad idea to join one.

After being a member there a few months I was asked to apply for their position as Music Minister. They offered it to me and I accepted.

I had never worked for a church before. What I came to find out is that it was more of a hassle than I had expected.

First of all, I had to get up very early each Sunday morning. Second, because I play the piano people were asking me to accompany them for special music, presuming that since I was already at church it wouldn't be a big deal. Unfortunately, it's more of a deal than people think. Singers want to rehearse, which of course takes time during the week. Then, just to make sure they've got it right, they'd say, "Let's meet a half hour early before the first service."

Trying to coordinate the music for two different services, oftentimes flying from the balcony where the organ stood, down near the altar to the piano to accompany someone and then flying again back up to the balcony for another piece to conduct was not church for me. I was putting in more hours than what the job description entailed. Since my talent was music and music was "fun," it was assumed that I would be thrilled to donate my time doing what I did for my profession. It became an unfulfilling job, especially on an Easter Sunday when my four-year-old daughter decided to vomit just before the first service began.

The ultimate discomfort occurred when a couple men in the church were vying for my attention in a romantic way, though my reason for joining a congregation was not to have a built-in dating service as part of its ministry. As I endured the unwanted interest and finally stood up for myself when they didn't seem to understand the word "no," admiration for me soon turned into antagonism. When I saw no end to it I resigned from my job.

I was still continually asked to play or sing for services. I had no desire to, and I politely declined. For some reason, that annoyed people.

But you're so talented, you should be sharing your gifts, don't you realize what God has given you, don't you see how we are being cheated out of your special talent....

It wasn't just the men who had been attracted to me who were belligerent. I became completely turned off by church by the presumption that I *should* be participating in a way I didn't wish to. I didn't need the aggravation or the reminder that not just a clergyman, but some parishioners can make church life difficult for a person. I found myself going back to the enjoyment of lazy Sunday mornings with no more church politics or men on the prowl to contend with.

One evening I was watching TV and the phone rang.

"Hi, Talia!" It was my best friend from high school, Caroline, who lived in Wisconsin, just an hour's drive from my home in St. Paul. "Say, how about you come to my church some Sunday and sing special music for our contemporary service?" Her husband played guitar and she knew the pastor would be okay with it as long as it was planned.

"No way..." I'd had enough wheedling from the Presbyterians.

She said, "Come on, it'll be fun and we'll have a great time!"

UGGGHHH, my automatic response thought. This would mean I'd need to be awake at an *ungodly* hour just to get ready and then drive for an hour, add maybe another half hour to find the place, and then add another half hour to do sound checks and get ready for the service. I was mentally calculating my ETA (Estimated Time of Alarm) while she talked about how the congregation would "*really, really* appreciate my music." Figuring this would be just a one-time situation, I unenthusiastically gave in.

Sigh. "Fine...I'll do it."

Some weeks later I managed to drag myself out of bed during the sunrise pink and peach and magenta and frankly, I didn't find anything awesome about it. I got the coffee going and started the grooming process. At any other time, I could be showered, dressed and find something to eat in forty-five minutes tops and fly out the door. Not so this morning. A couple weeks back I had made the mistake of allowing myself to be a model for a cosmetology competition. My stylist's specialty was chemicals and that meant coloring my hair. Naturally I was a light-brunette so I figured, hey, I'd get my hair colored for free, maybe spice it up a bit. Little did I expect we would go through eight processes over two days to turn my hair to a near platinum blonde. It was so porous I now had to stand for half an hour with a blow dryer even though my hairstyle was on the long side of a pixie cut. I would then need to curl every single dried-out strand to make it presentable so I wouldn't look as if a pile of hay were sitting on my head. Cursing both my stylist and myself that I had made this Sunday morning commitment I began the task of trying to make my face match my hair. The striking blonde completely washed out my Eastern European complexion so another twenty minutes was spent changing the colors of my face with foundation, shadows, liners, mascara, blush, powder and lipstick. I no longer resembled the walking dead. I emerged from the bathroom looking like a Ukrainian Marilyn Monroe going on a photo shoot.

I found the church and met Caroline near the front door. She had to do a double-take to make sure it was me.

Yes, I know, I'm blonde now and my face makes me look like a hooker; let's get on with the sound check.

Caroline took me by the arm to meet the band. I gave my usual hug to her husband Sven who eyed "the new me" with a dubious look. She introduced me to Tim the bass player. I-can't-remember-who was on the keyboard and the drummer, well, he didn't show up.

Shortly thereafter a tall man walked in. She introduced me to him as their pastor, Charlie. I started my sound check and noticed the pastor and Sven talking while looking straight at me. Being all glammed up like a New York lady-of-the-evening didn't seem to fit in with the small-town, casual atmosphere. I began to feel self-conscious, and after the sound check I grabbed Caroline and made a bee-line to the coffee pot.

Sitting at a table was a pretty woman who looked quite pale. Caroline introduced us. Her name was Jane, a friend of hers, and she was married to the pastor.

"How did your treatment go this week?" she asked of Jane.

By listening to the conversation I found out that she'd been diagnosed with cancer for the second time and had her first course of chemotherapy that week. Running past were two boys whom she introduced as her children, Troy and Spudly, using the younger's family nickname. Jane made an attempt to settle them down and bring them into the sanctuary for the service.

The service began, the band played, I sang my songs, everything went smoothly and the service was over. As we were putting away the sound system, Caroline piped up.

"We're all going to brunch and it's our treat." By all, she meant her family of four: the pastor, Jane and their two boys, Tim the bass player, and me.

I followed everyone to the restaurant and I was seated strategically next to Tim. He was single and the possibilities of Caroline trying to do a little match-making came to my mind. It might have worked had I not been driven to focus all my attention on Jane. Remembering my own mother going through cancer and ultimately not surviving, I couldn't take my eyes off of her. I watched as she forced herself to eat; how she talked gently to the boys; how her husband paid such attention to her. Poor Tim was trying to make conversation and I was about as interesting as the color beige. We finished brunch, said good-byes and I couldn't help but give Jane a hug. I hoped so very much that her treatment would work. I took a glance at the boys as they dashed out the door.

Dear God, don't let it happen to this family.

Over the next couple years I would take a drive to visit Caroline every few months or so. Invariably I would see Charlie as he and Sven worked on one household project or another. A couple times I saw Jane but as time went on she was becoming weaker and didn't venture out as much.

It was a bitterly cold January day. I walked into my house and saw my caller ID flashing. Panic hit me. Without even looking I knew what had happened. This type of precognition had occurred to me before. I checked the caller ID just to make sure it was Caroline who had phoned. I didn't even listen to her message. I simply called her back and asked her to tell me what had happened to Jane.

She'd had a stroke as a result of the cancer and treatment weakening her system and had passed away. She gave the times and dates of the visitation and funeral. My work schedule allowed me to drive there just as the visitation began and to stay for an hour or so.

I was one of the first to arrive. I went up to Charlie, hugged him and gave my condolences. I couldn't speak with him for too long as I saw the room was starting to get rather crowded and others were waiting patiently. I wasn't in the mood to sit so I strolled around the gathering room and eventually made my way into a hallway.

A small, inconspicuous room caught my attention. Two boys sat in there eating burgers and fries, watching TV. Their faces were blank. Troy and Spudly. They were even younger than I was when I lost my mom. My initial instinct was to run up to them and hold them. I wanted them to know I understood how painful it was and I would do anything to make things better for them. I also knew they would have thought I was some neurotic freak. They didn't see me; in fact, I don't think they even noticed what they were watching on TV. I turned around in the hallway only to start walking as fast as I could in a flood of tears. I felt as if I was right in the middle of my mother's funeral. It had been a little over a year since my breakdown. PTSD kicked in and I panicked.

Omygod, I've gotta get out of here...

I quickly walked over to Charlie and interrupted whoever was talking to him.

"I really need to leave. I just wanted to say good-bye." Tears were streaming down my face. He looked perplexed.

"You know, it's usually the family that gets as upset as you are," he pointed out.

"It's a long story. Maybe I'll share it with you someday."

I spent the entire drive home sobbing. At home I took an extra pill for anxiety to stop the shaking. I felt exactly the same as I did when my roommate in college surprised me for my birthday: out of control, terrorized. It was time to enter the void; a place where all I could do was sleep, be comforted by my therapist, and then sleep some more.

It took me two weeks to return back to work and even still, I did my job on auto-pilot. My saving grace was my dad. He reminded me that my anxiety symptoms would come in waves and when they did, not to be alarmed and think I was moving backward on my recovery. I declined invitations, did the best I could to raise Irina and slowly but surely over a period of a few months I began to feel normal again.

Many months had passed and near the Christmas holidays my daughter and I sat in our cozy TV room and settled ourselves to watch *Star Trek: The Next Generation* reruns, which became our mother/daughter/geek bonding time every weeknight. The phone rang and though we usually let the machine take a message, not letting anything get in the way of our sacred Trekkie hour, a commercial was running so Irina got up and answered the phone.

She whispered to me with her hand over the speaker. "It's for you. It's that Charlie guy from Wisconsin, Caroline's friend."

I'd been told by Caroline a few months back that he had started dating someone, so his phone call was a surprise. I tried to sound nonchalant.

"Hel-LOH-OH."

Damn, that wasn't nonchalant.

"Hi, Talia."

"Um...hi."

"A group of us are going out to dinner, Sven, Caroline and two other couples next week on Friday. Would you like to join us?"

"Uh...sure," I replied. We made some small talk, and I was to meet him at Caroline's home. I hung up and my daughter gave me a strange look.

"You've got a weird expression on your face," she said as she studied me. I was always transparent to her. "Don't you want to see the guy?"

"I do," I said, even though I was puzzled by his call. I would be lying if I said I hadn't found him attractive but I was cautious. Caroline had told me he was dating someone else. *Warning: Curveball.*

My daughter dismissed the situation and we went back to watching *Star Trek.* I'd had so many dates that ended after the first or second get-together I'm assuming she figured it was just another free dinner for me.

When I arrived at Caroline's, Charlie was waiting for me. Before we left the house Caroline mentioned he wasn't dating that particular woman anymore.

Second Warning: Rebound!

Let's be honest. We've all had those awful rebound dates, dates complaining about how they can't understand why their partners left them, what a bitch or SOB so-and-so was as we look at our watches and make the excuse that we need to get home because we have to be up early the next day.

I had nothing to worry about. The eight of us had a splendid time. Caroline and I bantered like we always did and Charlie joined in comfortably. During dinner I came to find out that he had spent some time in the Soviet Union in the 1970s. I mentioned to him there was a fabulous Russian restaurant in St. Paul and I was happy to repay the favor of dinner. He was a bit hesitant.

Oops...fastball.

I needed to remember he was just out of a short relationship and coupled with the grief I was sure he was still experiencing, I assumed there was a lot going on in his mind. Christmas was coming up and I knew the first holiday without Jane would be difficult. He asked if I wouldn't mind waiting until after the New Year. I let it go and figured I'd wait a few months to call.

In March we made plans to go to the restaurant I'd suggested. My daughter wanted to visit her friend Jody and spend the night with her the evening of our date. Her friend's father, Scotty, was a high school classmate of mine.

"So, what are you up to this weekend?" Scotty asked.

"I'm going out to dinner tonight."

"Who is he?" He beamed.

Like all my married friends, he was hoping I would find romance again.

"Some guy I met through Caroline," I responded casually.

"So...what does he do?"

"Right now he does electrical work, but he's a pastor on leave."

"A *WHAT!?* You have a date with a pastor? Bwahahahaha!"

No surprise in his response. I'm not the most pious person in the world. In fact, Scotty and I had shared a few evenings together in our younger years where our lucidity was in question. In a way I was wondering myself how I ended up going on a date with this guy. All the Norwegian pre-seminary students at my college were too theological for me. Charlie had a Scandinavian last name and every Swede or Norwegian I ever dated was emotionally elusive. Rather than confront an issue, the phone calls from the men I dated would simply stop.

The date went well. In fact, it went so well it was the best first date I'd ever had. The conversation was easy and he had a great sense of humor. There was also a bit of mischief about him and I liked that a lot. He made me feel that he was just a regular guy and I never worried that what I said to him would be offensive, given his profession. When I picked up my daughter the next day and told Scotty how successfully the evening had gone he just shook his head.

"Talia," he said, "the Church wouldn't know what to do with you."

I agreed.

The following Friday, I received a call from Charlie. He was in town doing some electrical work for his sister-in-law's parents who lived in a suburb near me. When we had gone out on our date the previous weekend he noticed my garage door was having difficulty opening and shutting. He wanted to know if I'd like him to come over and have a look at it.

DUH! Free manual labor! Someone handy with tools!

He poked and prodded and found some wire and fixed it as if he were McGyver. I've always told him that was the moment I thought I could fall in love with him.

As my relationship with Charlie grew, he didn't seem to have a problem with my quirks and unorthodox ways. Since he had taken a leave of absence from parish ministry to raise his boys, religion was never a subject we talked much about. We continued dating on a regular basis and our fondness slowly blossomed into love.

In an effort to make some changes in his and the boys' life, Charlie decided to sell his house and move to new surroundings. I knew this would be a difficult time for the three of them as they had always associated their home with Jane. I wasn't sure if it was appropriate for me to help them make the move, but after I offered, he was happy for the help. I hoped my presence would perhaps lighten the emotional load a little bit.

The morning of their move I was slow to wake up. Someone was shaking my leg. I heard a female voice.

"Wake up. You're needed."

My head was foggy and at first I thought it was Irina, but she was at her dad's and the voice didn't sound like her. I dismissed it and snuggled into my blankets to snooze a little longer; however, my leg was being shaken again, this time with much more effort. Again the voice spoke, even stronger.

"Wake up! You're needed!"

I turned to see who was disturbing my sleep and in a quick flash I saw Jane's face, and then the vision was gone. I woke up astonished.

Major curveball! Whoa – what the hell just happened?!

My thoughts went back to her visitation when I'd seen her boys sitting hopelessly eating burgers and fries and trying to watch TV. I felt so helpless then. I couldn't do anything to ease their pain. A strong impulse pulled me out of bed.

I got dressed and went to help them move. It was a peculiar day. Emotions were running high with Charlie and the boys, as well as with Caroline, who brought her family to help. I kept busy packing without saying much and spent the day pondering over my morning experience. I noticed I couldn't keep from smiling.

I realized that a new chapter was beginning in my life.

A Reality Check

Charlie and I knew very early on in our relationship that there was something special between us. We had open and honest communication and within six months we discussed marriage in the distant future. I was still a little gun-shy about embracing a permanent relationship with anyone, and we both knew the grieving process of losing Jane would take time for him and the boys.

It was Christmas morning. Irina was at her dad's and step-mother's house opening gifts with her three brothers in that blended family. I drove to Wisconsin to have Christmas dinner at one of Charlie's relatives.

I knocked on Charlie's door and no one was answering. I peeked in and found out why no one could hear me knocking. All three of them were yelling at each other.

"God, get away from me, you're always in my face. Dad, tell him to stop annoying me!"

"Stop acting so stupid, guys! Where the hell is the dessert I made?"

"No one told me the brownies were off limits!"

"Why do you think I got up at 6:00 in the morning to bake brownies, Troy?!"

"Geez, I was starving!"

"You're always starving! Eat a decent breakfast!"

"I told you it was stupid to eat them, dumbass!"

"Would you quit horsing around, we're already late!" By this time all four of us were getting into the car.

"We wouldn't be late if Spudly didn't spend an hour in the bath-room. There wasn't any hot water left for me to take a shower!"

"Stop using up all the hot water! You're not the only one in this fam-ily that needs to take a shower!"

The three of them kept on sparring and I was ready to blow a gas-ket. It was Christmas and they were spoiling it for me. This wasn't the first time I had witnessed this type of scenario among the three of them. I couldn't contain my frustration any longer.

"Everyone just SHUT UP! It's Christmas Day and you're acting like kindergartners!"

Charlie replied, "Yeah guys, quit yelling at each other!"

I was livid. "What do you mean, 'guys'? You're just as guilty as they are with your childish behavior!" By this time I was in tears. "I'm going into the house and I'm going to compose myself. I can live with a lot, but this type of behavior I can't live with! When I come back to the car, you will need to decide whether to be civil to one another or continue to act like a bunch of idiots. If you choose to continue this *fucking* behavior, you'll have to do it without me around!" I slammed the car door and went inside.

I walked into the bathroom to splash some water on my face and to wipe off the mascara that was streaking down my cheeks.

Omygod, what have I done?

I had given an ultimatum. Not only that, I dropped the f-bomb in front of the boys. I loved Charlie so much, yet over the years I discov-ered that sometimes love isn't enough. My nerves were on edge with their earlier scenario and I knew I would never be able to handle this type of chaos on a regular basis.

I took a deep breath and got into the car. There was complete silence as we drove. About a half hour into the drive Charlie asked me, "Do you want to talk about it?"

"No."

We spent the entire time at his aunt's house not saying a word to each other. When the festivities were over, the four of us got in the car and drove back in silence to their home. When we arrived, I got out of the passenger seat and said to Charlie, "Bye. I'm gonna go home."

"No, you're not. I won't let you leave until we've talked about this morning."

Unenthusiastically, I followed him into the house. Troy and Spudly quickly went into their respective rooms and shut their doors.

Charlie took me by the hands and sat me down on the sofa. "I'm so sorry about the way we behaved."

I sighed. "I'm sure you are. I'm just not sure I can handle all this antagonism among the three of you. I can't...I won't live with it."

There were tears in his eyes. "I love you so much. I don't want you to leave us."

I took a good long look at him and saw how his humility, his honesty, his love was so authentic. Christmas is hard for anyone who has lost a loved one, and I knew that loss very well. On the inside I was very forgiving and the tears in his eyes made me melt. Outwardly I remained stoic and said, "I'm counting on you to change this behavior. Otherwise, I'm out of here."

That Christmas morning was the only moment I had hesitations about spending my life with Charlie.

Did their behavior change significantly? Not really.

But my heart did.

Despite the pain of losing loved ones to death and divorce, I made the concrete choice to allow myself to be vulnerable with another human being again. All it took was the right person and the genius of two mental health professionals who were confident I would heal enough to wear my heart on my sleeve.

A year and a half later, Charlie and I were married.

I used to wonder what a person felt like marrying someone who was widowed, if they felt they were competing for a person's love, or if they wanted to erase all memories of the spouse who died. I didn't experience either of those things. As Charlie and I walked down the aisle together I recalled seeing the vision I had of Jane telling me, "Wake up, you're needed." With a bit of peculiarity, and yet with absolutely no fear I sensed someone else was walking along with us.

Things You Might Hear in a Pastor's Family

When Charlie and I got married, a co-worker was curious about my home life with my pastor husband and our kids.

"So...do you spend a lot of time talking about God?" she asked.

I laughed. "No, not really. You should hear some of the things pastors and their families say to one another."

"Like what?"

I began to reminisce:

"Let's use gasoline and see how high we can make this bonfire."
   - *PKs, ages 12 and 14*

"He's a Pastor, but he's not like a REAL Pastor."
   - *Future PK explaining to others how her irreverent mother ended up engaged to a Pastor*

"Don't yell at ME about my language. HE just told me to fuck off!"
   - *PK sibling defending herself against her brother*

"Don't freak out, it doesn't smell that bad."
   - *PK, after nuking pepper in the microwave for an experiment*

"Don't freak out, it doesn't smell that bad."
   - *PKs burning incense to cover up other smells*

"I want this out of the house *immediately*. Get rid of it!"

- Pastor to PK upon discovering a five-leafed plant in PK's room

"Do you know how fast you were going?"
- Police officer to PK

"Um...eighty, eighty-five?"
- PK's response, not realizing it was a rhetorical question

"I'm going to bring an African-American, Jewish guy and introduce him to Grandpa as my boyfriend..."
- Feisty PK's threat to stir up her racist and bigoted grandfather

"...and I'm bringing his brother..."
- Feisty PK's brother

"You spent $80.00 on cleaning products?! You don't even clean this house! Stop... buying...shit!"
- Pastor to PK after good-looking door-to-door salesperson walks away

"I hate you!"
- PK to Pastor's Wife

"I hate my family! I hate my kids! I hate my husband! I must have been insane to get married again!"
- Pastor's Wife to single friend

"Folks, you can take your child home now."
- Police officer to Pastor and Pastor's Wife after picking up PK for drinking and using illegal drugs

"What is this?"
- Pastor's Wife to nineteen-year-old PK after retrieving a liquor bottle from the trash

"Uh……"
> - *PK*

"How dare you have that bottle in the trash?! *(Pause)* Don't you know that this is supposed to be recycled?"
> - *Pastor's Wife, choosing her battles*

"It's too quiet around here."
> - *Pastor and Pastor's Wife in their empty nest*

"You go sit down; we'll clean up the kitchen."
> - *PKs after they have moved out*

The Call

In many Protestant denominations finding a pastor for a church occurs through what is known as the call process. Usually the council
of the church appoints willing members to form a call committee. In
the short time I attended the Presbyterian Church, many parishioners
were eager to be a part of the call of a new pastor. I'm a bit perplexed by
this exuberance and I'm hoping the reason for it is that people are committed to uphold their church, as opposed to participating for the sheer
sake of power and control. All I know is getting the majority of people
to serve on any other church committee can often be like pulling teeth.

The entire process from start to finish can last anywhere from
nine to eighteen months. The committee reads through the mounds of
paperwork supplied by pastoral candidates, discusses the pros and cons
of each one, listens to them preach at an outside church, has several
interviews with each, talks some more amongst each other and finally
reaches a decision on which pastor to call. There are many factors
in the decision-making for a call committee. Where do they see the
direction of their church going? What do they want to avoid from their
experiences of previous pastors? Can this candidate lead in a way that
upholds the mission and vision statements of the church?

Those are the obvious questions they ask of each other, but there
are more subtle considerations as well. How low a salary can be nego-
tiated? How many members will they gain or lose? Will this person
make enough changes to move our church in a positive direction yet
understand that we like to keep certain things the way they are?

When the call process began for the church which Charlie was eventually to serve as a full-time pastor, he sent the committee the requisite amount of paperwork and we waited for a response. After many weeks he received a phone call for an interview.

My husband is quite an extrovert and he can talk to anyone about anything, so I wasn't too concerned about the impression he would make. What you see is what you get. He was raised on a dairy farm and pretentions don't exist in rural Wisconsin.

After his interview, a huge packet of information came in the mail not just for him, but for the both of us. It was from the call committee.

I waited until he got home and then ripped through the envelope. Inside was literature from the Chamber of Commerce of the area. In the packet were names of realtors, community events, advertisements for places of business, a local newspaper, and various maps of the area. It was a charming place and it was surrounded by *millions* of lakes. Okay, not millions but at least a few dozen. The interview must have gone really well as they were enticing us with a stack of pamphlets of this delightful neighborhood. I was ecstatic about becoming a resident of this quaint, bedroom community!

Shortly afterward the committee asked both of us to have dinner with them, followed by another interview after the meal.

Okay, now they want to meet the wife.

We drove the thirty-five minutes and the closer we got the more nervous I became. I wanted desperately to make a good impression. We were to meet the group in the co-op apartment building of the call committee's chairperson, Carlotta Swanson. We arrived and Carlotta met us at the security door. With as much grace as possible I introduced myself as Talia and she replied, "Nice to meet you, ma'am."

Ma'am? No one calls me Ma'am. So then, what do I call her? Ma'am? Mrs. Swanson? Carlotta?

"Likewise," I quickly responded.

In her building is a community room and for the dinner four long tables were set in a square, complete with table settings. Everyone else on the call committee had already arrived and stuck name tags on their shirts. Place cards were also standing behind their place settings for dinner so Charlie and I could see their names. First and last names were written on both. On my name tag and place card I had only Mrs. Peterson written on them. I have never been one to feel comfortable being called Mrs. by anyone, so as I met everyone I introduced myself as Talia, hoping they would pick up on it. Eventually they did, but the entire time Charlie was addressed as "Pastor."

The meal progressed and was served in four courses, all by a wait staff. This was not a church pot-luck event with "hot-dishes," gelatin salad and seven-layer-bars. Slowly, the dinner became less official and everyone warmed up to us. Little by little, my persona was showing through and my jitters abated.

"So, what kind of work are you involved in?" they asked me.

I went on to tell them I was a marketing manager at the time, but most of my working years had been spent in the entertainment field of music, theatre and some film and video. I was eager to get back into the arts when my husband was back to working fulltime in the ministry. They asked about my church upbringing and current church and I started by telling them about St. Stephen's. I quickly skimmed over the churches I'd attended after St. Stephen's, four of them with three different denominations. I received some confused looks and I could feel the heat rise to my face. This was a Lutheran church with families who had been members for many generations, probably since the Swedes established it in the late 1800s.

They asked what prompted my choice to change memberships and become inter-denominational. I had to think quickly so I mentioned that I had been immersed in the Lutheran Church when I attended a reputable Lutheran college in Minnesota known for its strong, sacred choral tradition and was asked to cantor the sung liturgy several times. Nods of approval. I passed on admitting when my four requisite semesters of choir were over I quit choir and instead took afternoon naps. Or that once I had no choral responsibilities for worship I didn't bother setting my alarm on Sunday mornings. I also conveniently skipped over the years I spent married to my first husband and my daughter's baptism in a Roman Catholic Church, which we rarely attended.

I segued into my membership in the Presbyterian Church. I attempted to circumvent the fact that I was the choir director there for a few years, but the committee had already caught wind of that information through Charlie's initial interview. The fact that I was hired for a music position in a church fascinated them. Unfortunately for me, they were entering uncomfortable territory.

Please don't ask why I left the position. I really don't want to get into the sordid details.

They didn't ask. I dodged that bullet and hoped the subject would not come up again.

After dinner, Carlotta Swanson came up to me and said, "We're having the interview now so I'll take you to my apartment." She was brisk and I followed as she walked rapidly with purpose.

Wait. I thought this was a gathering for both of us. They want me to leave.

I was brought into her apartment, chatting graciously while baffled as to why I was being quarantined. She showed me a selection of magazines I could read and then left me stranded.

This is not good. They want to talk about things I'm not supposed to hear, and if I'm not supposed to hear them, what are they? Do all spouses leave at this point, or is it just me?

The anxiety wouldn't leave and for forty-five minutes I sat in one of Carlotta's chairs, not reading, not using the bathroom, which I desperately needed to, just kept rocking back and forth, back and forth and waited as the sound of her clock ticked, ticked, ticked. She finally appeared with the same authority and brought me back to the community room.

"What was that all about?" I muttered to Charlie under my breath.

"Nothing," he said, "just church-talk."

The evening came to an end and the members of the call committee were kind and thankful for our time. As each one took my hand I gave everyone a small, warm hug, not too demonstrative, but it was something natural for me to do.

Weeks later, a letter came from the church:

Dear Pastor Peterson,

We wish to thank you for your interest ... (Etcetera, etcetera...) and at this time we release you from further discussion.

Sincerely,
Carlotta Swanson

"WHAAAAT???!!! They 'release' you from further discussion?! What kind of *bullshit* is that?! What was that packet of information about, giving us names of realtors and coffee shops and antique stores and seducing us to the community? You don't just send a bunch of crap and dangle the intention of hiring you, make us fall in love with the area and then get *released* from discussion!"

It had to be the hugs. They hated them.

No Scandinavian in Minnesota hugs someone they don't know. That much I'd learned in college. I had broken the cardinal rule of Swedish personal space.

I can't remember what Charlie even said, I was so enraged. I knew in my heart they were giving up on the wrong person.

A couple months later in the fall I joined Charlie for Sunday service at the small church where he was serving as interim pastor. We were to leave from there to spend two days at a leadership conference. We were ready to get away from it all to a beautiful retreat center in northern Wisconsin, just as the leaves were in the peak of their color.

I was about to go inside the church when I saw a van pulling into the parking lot. Out came the call committee with whom I'd had dinner who *dared* to "release" my husband from further discussion. I scampered inside the church and found a seat far away from them. The entire service I looked at them with beady eyes, mentally shooting poison darts for their refusal to hire my husband. When the service was over they asked him if they could speak with him privately and their looks at me implied "you're not invited to this conversation."

I sat in a pew waiting, fuming that I was cast aside again. Before I had the opportunity to talk with any of them after the meeting, Charlie found me and they had already left. We got into the car and I slammed my door. We drove away in silence and stopped in the nearest town to eat lunch, with which I had two glasses of wine.

"So, what did *they* want?" I finally asked him with incensed sarcasm.

He stayed calm. "They all came up to me and looked a little sheepish. They asked if I would accept their offer as senior pastor."

"Sheepish? You're *damned* right they ought to be sheepish, first *releasing* you from further discussion and now coming back to realize what a mistake they had made!"

I kept on with my litany of how obtuse they were to not hire him in the first place and he just let me drone on and on about the situation and drink through my fury. I finally stopped and realized he never told me if he had accepted their offer.

"What did you tell them?"

"I told them I had to talk it over with my wife first."

Ah, my sweet husband. Always thinking of me, always wanting to be sure I was happy. During this process he had kept his cool while I took everything so personally.

On our first Sunday at church Carlotta came up to me, gave me a big hug, smiled and said, "Welcome, dear. We're so glad you're with us."

Over the years I have come to know Carlotta as a close confidante. You see, she also was married to a pastor and knows first-hand the ups and downs of being The Pastor's Wife. Despite her Swedish last name she was born into a family of Italians and has a fiery disposition about her that I have come to admire. As we joked about the call process and my reaction she gave me some insight as to what was happening on their end.

"We went back and forth about the call and I can imagine God was just sitting back thinking, "You go about your silly little business and disputes and if you had just allowed the Spirit to move you in the first place the right pastor would have been here that much sooner."

That still, small voice is in all of us. Sometimes it takes us a while to trust it, and then once we do, sometimes we just need to be patient with others who need the time to listen to it. And then when you're someone who is impassioned like me, purging it out loud is the most therapeutic thing a person can do.

The Honeymoon Period

In any job there is always a honeymoon period where a new employee gets the royal treatment upon arrival. When the employee is a new pastor the attention is magnified.

During this "getting to know you" phase the church is all abuzz to meet The Pastor and in our case, The Pastor's Wife as well. It's like an arrival of two new babies to the congregational family. People can't wait to see them, can't wait their turn to talk to them, put on their biggest smiles and try to cozy up to get on their good side.

Since we were commuting from the suburbs I would come early in the morning with Charlie, attend the first worship service, have coffee with the parishioners afterward, and then usually find someone who was willing to sit and talk with me through the second service. I got to know quite a few people in those first few weeks and they were extremely gracious. We often received invitations for brunch or a full dinner at a parishioner's home after church.

I had been combing through my closet and noticed that my sense of fashion was on the avant-garde side. I owned only a couple items that were trendy and what I felt were considered church appropriate. It was January and the after-Christmas sales were now flashing "CLEARANCE!" I entered a small clothing boutique at the local mall, one I usually avoided as their prices, even on clearance, were higher than I was willing to pay. I thought I'd just take a peek, maybe I could find something chic yet inexpensive.

I don't know what happened to me. I suddenly lost my bargain mind-set and was hauling all sorts of beautifully textured woolen skirts and matching tops off the racks and into the dressing room in a maniacal state. I justified buying three complete outfits with accessories by noting how many hundreds of dollars I was saving. My daughter was shopping with me and she couldn't believe I was being this indulgent. I had taught her the ins and outs of bargain shopping and how to still maintain a fabulous sense of style. As a fashion expert since she was three years old, even she had to admit her mother looked top drawer.

The very next Sunday I came walking into church with my straight-lined purple tweed skirt, an asymmetrical mauve sweater, purple Mary Jane heeled shoes and matching jewelry. Never mind the fact I over-spent on my clothing budget; I needed to make a good impression!

I made my way around the crowd before the service began and talked with people I had already gotten to know. I was in a conversation with one woman who was on the call committee when we were joined by another woman. Introductions were made, and my new friend decided to give me some information.

"You *know*," she said, "*I heard* The Pastor was called to this church because you are musical and would be an additional asset to the music ministry."

At this point, the woman from the call committee looked horrified. I had some idea as to what was going on in this poor woman's mind.

"What are you thinking?! We don't bring someone on board to see what we can squeeze out of his wife, even if that thought crossed our minds!"

The brat in me was dying to upset the apple cart.

I looked at the other woman, raised my eyebrows and said, "Oh, you mean hiring him so the church could get a two-for-one?"

The woman from the call committee responded, completely blushed with embarrassment.

"Well of course we found out that Talia was musically talented, but we don't base our decision on the gifts The Pastor's Wife could bring.

Certainly, if she wishes to participate musically in the church, we'd be delighted." I was impressed with her answer.

"That's not what I *heard.*" The woman was adamant she had the goods on the inner gossip.

To put the woman from the call committee at ease, I remained polite but was very much to the point with the potential gossip-monger.

"What, may I ask, do you do for a profession?"

"I'm a social worker."

"Oh, so you volunteer in that capacity here at church?"

"Well, no...."

"You don't?" She didn't say anything after that, just stared speechless.

"Ah...well, I would suggest that whoever your source is who told you the church believes they received a 'two-fer,' you might want to let that person know that he or she is horribly mistaken."

Didn't make a new friend that day.

The bells were ringing, announcing that worship was to begin, so I said, "Nice to meet you. I'd better get inside the sanctuary." I walked down the center aisle and sat in one of the front pews.

After worship I gathered with the parishioners for coffee. I saw the woman I'd been introduced to and had some guilt gnawing at me.

Okay, maybe I was a little snarky with this woman. I'll be nice.

"Hi," I said to her with a smile.

I received a nasty glare.

"I noticed," she said smugly, "when you walked down the center aisle, all the men turned their heads to see your legs with that skirt of yours."

I looked at what she was wearing and noticed it was a jumper, almost to her ankles.

Skirt of mine? The length is just above the knee-cap! I spent more money trying to look presentable than I should have! Why don't you just tell me you think my skirt is too damned short, lady?!

After composing myself from her comment I quipped, "Well, I guess I'll just have to wear this skirt more often."

I received an encore on the nasty glare.

Charlie and I drove home in silence and my thoughts were that I wasn't feeling all that optimistic about this new role as The Pastor's Wife. We had been at the church for only a few months or so and I was already struggling with the notion that I needed to live up to someone else's expectations. At home, I asked him to sit down.

"Charlie, you know the kind of person I am. You also know how much work I've put into therapy and how hard it was to destroy the old tapes I had running through my head about what I 'should' be doing. I feel as if I'm obliged to act or dress a certain way at church. I also feel that I can't speak my mind, give my outlook on how I feel spiritually, or talk about what's important to me socially or politically. I don't want to be stifled and I also want to support you and what you feel called to do. I feel as if I'm being pulled in two different directions."

He looked at me and smiled. "Sweetheart, I married you for *you*, not what a congregation expects you to be. I want you to be yourself. I'm called to serve everyone in the congregation and I keep my personal viewpoints in check because I'm serving a wide variety of people. This call is mine, not yours. If you don't feel as if you can be who you are then this isn't the right place for us.

"Seriously?"

"Seriously."

"It wouldn't bother you if I put DFL stickers on my car or talk about my socially progressive views, or organize a tai chi class, even though some people think it's Eastern propaganda blasphemy?

Charlie laughed. "If that's what you really want to do, I'm certainly not going to try to stop you."

With tears of gratitude, I held him tight. "I love you so much."

That afternoon I returned the two unworn outfits to the overly priced boutique. I went to the department store where I usually shopped and bought the loudest clothes I could find and large, colorful bling for accessories.

The following Sunday I walked into church splashed in purple and orange and magenta, outshining any sunrise. Jumper Lady was looking at me and whispering to someone seated next to her.

It was the beginning of the end of the honeymoon period and I didn't care.

The brat is back, and she ain't goin' anywhere!

The Apartment

After starting his new call, Charlie commuted thirty-five miles to the church for more than a year. Our youngest graduated from high school and our house in the suburbs took nine months to sell. Those were long days for him, as he stayed at church if there was an evening meeting. So once the house sold, we were exhausted and the ordeal of coordinating a purchase at the same time was unappealing, to say the least. We decided we would rent a place near the church and take our time looking for a home to buy. While he was working, I scoured the neighborhoods for apartments, hoping we could find one that would allow us to have a month-to-month lease.

I found a few. One was fairly nice, but the cigarette smell went through to the third layer of wallpaper.

Another one was quite inexpensive. I passed on it as even the cockroaches weren't interested in residing there.

I was feeling a bit disgruntled as I drove back to the church. I would need to return another day to search again. I walked into my husband's office and he had some news.

"Say, I heard there's a place available for rent, two bedrooms, twelve-hundred square feet and we can arrange a month-to-month lease!"

"Really?" I exclaimed. "Can I see it today?"

"You can," he said, "but you might not like the location."

"How far is it from the church?" I asked.

"About three, four miles."

"What's not to like?" I questioned. "It's close and you can actually drive home for dinner if you have an evening meeting. So, where is it?"

He told me, and gave me the number of the building owner. I saw the apartment, the landlord quoted us a very reasonable rent and it included air-conditioning, heat, electricity, wi-fi and cable. As for the location, it was on a frontage road next to the highway, but there were no windows facing the traffic. What luck! It was perfect for us.

I'd see people at church and say, "You really should come over to our place and we can have coffee together." I was ready to entertain yet everyone, it turned out, would make a suggestion to meet at the local coffee house just down the road from the apartment.

"Are you sure?" I'd ask. "It's really no trouble."

Nobody wanted me to go to the trouble.

For the next eight months we had a comfortable place to relax from our day with peace and quiet. Occasionally, the landlord would host large groups of people, but they never stayed long, and always left at a reasonable hour of the night.

Our landlord and the others in the building were great. When he saw us in the parking garage, he'd offer us an imported beer from a mini-fridge and we'd shoot the breeze with him. Once, he was barbequing and invited us for burgers and beer. The rest of the people in the building came and joined us. We watched the Minnesota Twins game together and agreed that we should do this again.

After several months of looking at houses, we finally found one. The landlord was sad to see us go. We were great renters, he said, and we reciprocated by telling him we couldn't have asked for a better landlord.

As Charlie and I were leaving for the last time, I looked back and was sorry no one ever came to visit us. It was a nice place.

Maybe the fact it was above the funeral parlor made them feel uncomfortable.

※❂※

It's interesting to observe how the culture in the United States reacts to death or anything surrounding it. The apartment we lived in was completely separate from the funeral home, an add-on above the garage with a private stairway. The idea of walking past the company van and hearse to get to our place was unnerving for people and I was genuinely surprised. People living in the area had been to this funeral home, probably numerous times, to pay respects to the families of people they loved, or even their own loved ones and never had an issue entering the visitation room. Most everyone believed those who had died were in a better place, yet my invitation to come over for coffee made their hair stand on end and some would literally shiver.

"Dead people live there," they'd remark, and I would remind them they don't *live* there – they're dead.

"It would creep me out to live among spirits" was another statement I often heard. I would assure them there were no apparitions haunting me.

After receiving these uncomfortable reactions to my living quarters I decided to observe people when they attended a visitation. Friends make the gracious effort of going for the sake of the grieving family and to somehow "be there for them." They take the obligatory pause at the casket or urn, sometimes say a prayer, sometimes stand quietly, and then quickly leave the area of the deceased. They look at the memorabilia out of respect for the family members who have put the shrine of the deceased together, but don't generally linger on any pictures or personal items.

Some will cry for the family members. Rarely have I seen people truly grieve because they too have lost that person.

With the exception of New York City, where you can sit in a crowded restaurant and sob like crazy without anyone paying attention to you, most people in the United States will not openly weep unless it's at an assigned, appropriate time. They might cry at moments, such as seeing the deceased for the first time in a casket, listening to a eulogy, standing at the cemetery or consoling a family member. So many people have been drilled to internalize their grief. I have on one occasion seen a family member of the deceased berate another for not pulling herself together to be strong to welcome the guests who were there. I've witnessed other people quickly divert a conversation and flee so others wouldn't see them break down into tears.

My most notable experience living at the funeral home was my first contact with a casket in the garage. The staff had prepared the body for viewing and they were arranging the visitation room. Reactively, I was ready to race upstairs to the apartment but I realized a casket in the garage might be something I'd encounter again so I'd better get used to it. I slowly made my way over to it. It was opened slightly, enough for me to see the deceased. I stayed there for a number of minutes. I took a good long look and realized this body was not a person anymore. Dead is dead. No life, no soul, no misery, no pain, nothing, an empty shell. What that person was in life was no longer there with me.

Throughout those eight months I witnessed a variety of visitations. Since I lived there from spring through December I often spent my time sitting on the small deck off the living room. In some instances the parking lot looked as if a party was going on. An occasional flask or six-packs from coolers would pop open. People who normally didn't smoke would light up, cigars often being passed around. For one evening, people would throw caution to the wind, not caring who saw them smoke or drink in a public place. Whether they drank for themselves or part of a toast to the person who died, it was a moment of necessary relief.

The tradition of a gathering with food after a funeral service doesn't happen because the family feels obligated to feed the visitors. People bond over food, happy or sad. The idea of Jesus inviting his disciples to have supper with him before being condemned to death is something I can relate to. The Church embraces it as the Sacrament of the Eucharist. For me, if I knew I was going to die the next day, I personally would want the people closest to me to share an extraordinary meal the night before.

At the end of my stay at the apartment I was privy to one last visitation while we were moving. I didn't know the deceased or the family.

I lugged boxes from the apartment to my new home, back and forth. I had a long day of moving and it was already dark outside. I was tired and decided I would make one last haul to the house. Things were winding down from the visitation and I noticed one woman in particular. She was busy saying goodbye to those who'd come. I drove off to unload the last boxes for the day and when I returned to the funeral home the woman was still in the parking lot, offering a few remaining good-byes and finally speaking with the funeral home director.

As I went up the stairs and into the apartment I could hear crying from outdoors. I looked out the window and there was this same woman, standing next to the only car left in the parking lot, sobbing her heart out. I quickly opened up a bottle of wine, threw on my coat, grabbed a couple of glasses, and walked down to where she stood. I poured for the both of us and she accepted it graciously. She was about to say something, but I shook my head and said, "Unless you want to talk, don't feel obligated. You've done enough talking today."

We clinked glasses and simply stood there and sipped without a word. I never did find out her name. I cried along with her, taking the time to grieve the people I had lost in my own life.

Sometimes saying nothing can speak volumes.

Spiritual Gifts

When most people join a church, there are numerous ways they can volunteer, such as teaching Sunday school, becoming part of the worship team, working with local and international missions – there are many ways to keep active in the church community. My husband's church also has different committees on which to serve, and out of those committees there might be sub-committees that focus on specific ministerial responsibilities.

I'm not a committee person. I hate meetings. When I was working in marketing a meeting meant I couldn't work on my list of at least fifty tasks that needed to be taken care of. We all know that in meetings there are always one or two people who like to ramble on from one tangent to another, which my daughter aptly describes as "The Drunk Driving of Conversation." For me, social time is social time and work time is work time and a meeting should have an agenda, a time limit, let's stay on the subject, finish, and get back to work or go home. That's my idea of a meeting. More often than not it's not going to happen that way.

Bible studies are just another meeting for me. I always pictured Bible studies to be a place where you read scripture and have great thought-provoking discussions that leave you feeling enlightened and recharged. But every Bible study I've been to (four, to be exact) has provided me with a sheet of paper with bullet points to follow. No thought-provoking discussions. I was in another marketing meeting.

That being said, I was at a loss as to how I would spend my time contributing my "spiritual gifts" at our new church.

The idea of spiritual gifts for me has always been a touchy subject. I've already spoken of my lack of desire to use my music profession for church. The insistence from others that this is something I *should* do just because they want me to do it doesn't fly with me anymore. I had spent plenty of time in therapy deprogramming myself from the "shoulds." So, whenever someone uses the word "should" on me I feel there is a guilt trip lurking in the wings.

One day Charlie remarked, "I noticed when I facilitate the adult forum in between services, you don't come to participate." It's not that I didn't want to support him and his call to teach. But hearing him say forum made me think of the tedious leadership-yay-yay-rah-rah events I was subjected to with 2'x3'-sized poster papers taped across every square inch of wall available. I even experienced the same shudder at the word forum that encompassed me when I was holed up in a conference room.

"Uh...I'm using my spiritual gift."

"What? Your gift of drinking coffee?" I gave him a smirk.

With a bit of sarcasm I came back with, *"No, love of my life.* My spiritual gift of "conversation'."

He didn't comment to my response. I didn't find it convincing myself when I had said it.

Yet Sunday after Sunday I would chit-chat with someone and more often than not my husband would be ready to lock up the church and I'd still be gabbing away or getting to know someone by finding out more about them. I realized there was something to this spiritual gift of conversation after all. In the past, because everyone felt my musical gifts were meant for the Church, I had spent too many Sundays trying to get a choir to watch me direct instead of me watching them keep their noses in their music. Or, I had flailed my arms too many times, gesturing to children to stop being shy and sing louder when I knew they could vocalize at astounding decibels at any other given moment. By being preoccupied with what I thought was my spiritual gift I was missing out on what I loved doing most – getting to know people.

Little did I ever think that my gift of socializing would be confirmed when some years back I reconnected with a friend from high school at a reunion. Several months later we saw one another by chance and she invited me to her house for dinner and fireworks for the 4th of July.

Let me just say, this woman is the ultimate mom. She was raising five children; one being a niece after her brother had died. Add the fact she was doing this as a single parent and making the best out of what could have been a difficult situation. She had a vegetable garden, flower gardens everywhere, the house was decorated for the summer, she sewed her own window treatments, was a marvelous cook and she ran an in-home daycare. Now *that* woman would have made an ideal Pastor's Wife!

I said to her five-year-old, "Boy, you have a really great mom. I'm a terrible mom. She does so many things around the house that I just don't care to do."

He looked at me and asked, "So, don't you garden?"

"Nah, not really. I plant just a few flowers in the boxes that are attached to the house."

"Do you cook?"

"Only because I'd starve if I didn't."

"Do you bake?"

"Nope. Chips Ahoy cookies and Hostess cupcakes are what my daughter and I eat for dessert."

"Do you sew?"

"Oh my goodness, you'd never want to wear anything I've sewn! I'd probably make the hole your head is supposed to fit through too small. You'd end up being a ghost every Halloween and even then I'd probably cut the holes for your eyes, nose and mouth in the wrong places."

"Do you decorate?"

"Well, yes, but only for Christmas. And then it's just a tree and a few trimmings."

He looked at me for a while and suspiciously asked, "Do you like kids?"

I smiled and said, "I love kids! I think kids are the greatest!"

"Well, then, *you're* a great mom!"

Smart kid.

Many years later when my husband took his call, I reminded myself of the conversation I had with that adorable child. I also remembered him hugging me at the end of the night and asking me to come back and visit again. We shared the spiritual gift of conversation and I came home that evening feeling more validated as a parent, despite my lack of domesticity

No one really knows what happens when you take the time to talk with someone. A person doesn't need to give advice, or try to solve any problems, because simply listening to another person makes that person feel important. More importantly, I believe that the listener often benefits even more than the speaker. Listening encourages me to shut up for a while and stop being so narcissistic.

I love using my spiritual gift of conversation and I particularly love what I take away from it. And just to keep me humble, my family endearingly points out my motoring skills when I perchance get ahead of myself and maneuver into the "Drunk Driving of Conversation."

As I think about it, more than likely it was me everyone rolled their eyes at in my marketing meetings.

Discovering the Tribes

When I started attending Protestant churches all of them were much larger than St. Stephen's Ukrainian Greek Catholic Church. At St Stephen's we had certain friends we knew better and socialized with, but for the most part, what affected one person affected the entire congregation. Everyone chipped in without hesitation to keep the congregation going.

There was a high level of frustration for me in my attempt to become active in one of the many ministries available to participate in to develop social connections. Just because I might share the same interest with a group of people in a congregation didn't mean I was able to infiltrate into their close-knit group. I thought being married to a pastor would give me an easier ticket for entry. The honeymoon period is a "teaser" where most of the congregation gives The Pastor's Wife the impression that she's invited to be a part of some social or work group; but just like any other organization, some people in a church are quite content regarding the status quo on what, how and with whom they do whatever it is they do.

There are many imaginative words to describe a social group: circle, community, guild, clique, coalition, alliance, country club, union, sorority/fraternity, even syndicate. Most pastors and their spouses would agree with me that any one of these words typifies a congregation at one point or another.

Being an information geek, I went to my computer and typed in Wikipedia. Man, I love Wikipedia. You have a question about something, type the question in on its home page and *voila*, you can know anything there is to know about everything.

As I investigated Social group one word stood out: Tribe. Before going through the text I looked up the word Tribe in various online dictionaries and found one definition that resonated with me:

A social division in a traditional society consisting of families or communities linked by social, economic, religious, or blood ties

As I began reading about Tribes in Wikipedia, the unnerving part was I wanted to click on all the highlighted words before getting to the end of the page. I began to digress from the initial subject, but in the process I had accumulated a wealth of information by weaving through many of the highlights:

Tribe: See also: **Social Unit**.

A **social unit** consists of a number of individuals interacting with each other with respect to:

1. Common motives and goals
2. An accepted **division of labor**
3. Established status (**social rank** or dominance in relationships)
4. Accepted norms and values with reference to matters relevant to the group
5. Development of accepted **sanctions** (praise and punishment) if and when norms are respected or violated.

Sanctions: mechanisms of **social control**.
Social control: See also **Informal social control**.
Informal social control: Informal sanctions may include **shame, ridicule, sarcasm, criticism** and **disapproval**. In extreme cases sanctions may include **social discrimination** and **exclusion**.

As you can see, Wikipedia can become distracting yet sociologically fascinating.

Instead of looking at what might be the evident tribes in churches, such as the council or groups that support missions or worship or hospitality, I made close observations of tribes that weren't listed regarding church participation.

The Gossip Tribe

They're good at that childhood game "Telephone" where you whisper something into someone's ear and pass it down. By the time it gets to the last person the original statement is distorted. Here's a good example:

"The Pastor's Wife looks a little tired today."

"I heard The Pastor's Wife is always tired."

"I heard that The Pastor's Wife's eyes were really bloodshot yesterday."

"The Pastor's Wife always has bloodshot eyes; do you think she might be drinking?"

"I heard The Pastor's Wife is always tired because she is pregnant. And she's drinking while carrying the child!"

"Oh, my goodness, what is she thinking?!"

"Ssshhh...here she comes..."

"Hello, Talia, how are you today?"

"Great!"

"Well, that's good. Anything new with you?"

"Nope."

"Uh huh...well, have a nice day..."

"I wonder when The Pastor's Wife will start to show?"

This of course could go on *ad nauseum*, but you get the picture.

In case you were wondering – I never did show.

The Kitchen Tribe

I have to say the **Kitchen Tribe** in most churches is very efficient. The tribal members are happy to take charge. "You say you'd like to help? No really, we can handle it. No, *really*. No, *R-E-A-L-L-Y.*"

I have no idea where anything is located in the church kitchen. The **Kitchen Tribe** is always on hand to find it for me.

The Tribe can take a sigh of relief now that we have automated coffee machines. I can't mess with the ratio of coffee to water anymore to make it stronger.

To be fair, the **Kitchen Tribe** is always looking out for my well-being. When I was diagnosed with celiac, which requires me to eat gluten-free, the tribe always has a salad or casserole available without gluten in it. No one from a **Kitchen Tribe** would ever allow anyone to walk out of a pot luck meal hungry.

By the way, I did find out how to make the coffee stronger with the new machines. Just one or two extra presses of a button...

We've Always Done It This Way Tribe

Let's face it. For some people change is a four-letter word.

"What was good for our great-grandparents at this church is good enough for all of us. Why are we using piano accompaniment instead of organ music? Why do we need new hymnals? The old hymns from two centuries back are just fine and we *like* it that way."

"And what is this clapping business in church? We're here to pray reverently and solemnly. This isn't a performance. What is this business about the Spirit moving someone to applaud? It's just not traditional and isn't the Spirit the reason we have Pentecostal and Baptist churches?"

"Why are we having outdoor services in the summertime? I've put my hard-earned money into this building and we should use it, dammit!"

"And what's this idea of 'home churches'? Can't some people get off their lazy asses and make it to a church service?"

Interestingly enough, the Gospels write about Jesus teaching outdoors and at dinner parties in people's homes.

Pastor, Wouldn't It Be Great If We... Tribe

Some people have an abundance of suggestions on how their church can be improved. So when The Pastor asks these people to come up with a plan on said improvement, they don't make a plan. And then they get mad when The Pastor doesn't do anything about their suggestion.

I Will Call You About Church Stuff Even When You're On Vacation Tribe

Okay folks, when my husband works sixty hours or more a week to serve his congregation, vacation is vacation, and he, and especially I, do not want to receive calls about anything church related. People do not contact their accountants, chiropractors or hairdressers when they are on vacation and everyone needs to know this also must apply to their pastors. Their ministry is demanding and the purpose of a vacation is to get away from *anything* related to work. These are certain phone messages and texts my husband has received while on vacation:

"I wanted to let you know I'm having my routine colonoscopy done. Would you pray for me?"

"I've never facilitated this meeting. How long should it last?" *Until you've completed the agenda, perhaps?*

"Oh my goodness *(gasp)*, I'm in the middle of this new project at church *(gasp)* and I know you're on vacation, and I really *(gasp)* don't want to bother you even though you said I could talk to a council person *(gasp)* if I had any questions, but you might think this is important... *(gasp)*"

"I know you're on vacation, but you're not out of town, so I figured you're not really on vacation."

There is something that *always* needs a pastor's attention when he or she is on vacation.

Hell froze over.

The Passive-Aggressive Tribe

For anyone who was born and raised in the upper Midwest, you know exactly what I mean by the **Passive-Aggressive Tribe**. Minnesota Nice is an accurate way of describing the people who live in this state. It's also a behavior people use when they don't want to confront someone face-to-face. Some people will circumvent what they actually feel and say that everything is fine with them when it isn't. I can't even count the number of times a person has said one thing to me, then bitched about whatever it was that bothered them about me to someone else.

If you have a problem with me, please let me know what it is without me feeling as if you and I are playing a game of cat and mouse. My ego may suffer for a few moments, but I will most definitely appreciate your candor.

There's a Problem with *You* Tribe

These are the excluders:
- *She* smokes, so *she* shouldn't be allowed to teach Sunday School to children
- We can't put this person in charge of the nursery; *she* is on anti-depressants
- *You're* not welcome to come because everyone in this group is married and *you're* single (I know this one quite well. I was that D-word once, remember?)
- We can't have this person's funeral here; *he's* not a member
- I've always done this job at church myself and I don't have the time to teach *you* how to do it
- We shouldn't encourage this woman to come back; I hear *she*, you know, "likes" women

Sure, I'll Help Tribe

In every church setting there are about 10% of the people who do 90% of the work.

There are both good and bad aspects to this. On one hand, the work has to get done by someone, and those who support the pastor want to be sure that she or he doesn't become burnt out. On the other hand, it makes the rest of the congregants idle as they know this particular tribe will pick up the slack.

The Sanctimonious Tribe

I was talking with my husband about how I had a block in expressing myself with this tribe. "I know what's inside my head, but I can't quite find the right words for it."

He said, "I'm sure it'll come to you when you least expect it." I left the room to get back to the manuscript.

Before returning to my task at writing I went online.

Lo and behold!

A member of the **Sanctimonious Tribe** had graced me with his presence by posting on social media:

I believe in Jesus Christ and have accepted Him as my personal Savior. I challenge all believers to share this. In the Bible it says, if you deny me in front of your peers, I will deny you in front of my Father at the gates of Heaven. This is simple...if you love God and you are not afraid to show it, share this...No shame!

That's it? Share a posting and I'm in? How did I not know this?

No shame? Did I read that correctly? It sure sounds manipulative to me.

As a favor:

Would everyone who finds these emails or postings annoying *please* raise their hands?

Wait...don't go on yet...I haven't finished counting.

Look, I realize in many cases people's religious intentions are good and many folks are touched by Jesus or by other religions and want to proclaim it to the world. That's not how my relationship with God works, but if it does for someone else, I think that's great. My own husband proclaims it with our congregation on a daily basis, and especially through his Sunday sermons. I continue to follow my dad's advice and remember that how and what people believe is holy to them and their outward expression of their spirituality may be what God has called them to do.

There are some in this vociferous group, however, who believe they have the inside scoop of what is going on in God's mind. Some sanctimonious Christians will blame other world religions, minorities, homosexuals, separation of church and state, family curses, women in the workplace, menstrual cycles and Eve for the earthquakes, hurricanes, tornadoes, mass murders or any tragedy that occurs.

Except for war. God is on our side, and it's a straight man's job to do it.

This variety of talk burns me to no end. I find it conniving, a form of religious abuse, xenophobic, and worst of all, degrading to God. It is no better than the Pharisees who tried to manipulate Jesus to unsuccessfully catch him in a "gotcha" moment. I find it interesting how clearcut this **Sanctimonious Tribe** can be about other people's sins, yet if they have been caught in a sin themselves they take out their God-in-a-pocket, tell people they have repented and that God has told them they are forgiven. How convenient.

To those who feel the urge to use manipulation, sanctimony and shame as a means of evangelism, my opinion is you're more than likely turning off a lot more people than bringing them closer to God – at least the God you're portraying.

※※

I have to say, it was amusing to write about the idiosyncrasies of the tribes you can find at *any* church. I could laugh or jab at a group of people at their expense and, let's be honest; a person is going to find these tribes and many more in society, too. Individuals, communities, leaders in our country, even groups who are seeking justice and doing good works in this world like to gossip, are territorial, are stubborn to change, look for other people to do their work, disrespect boundaries, seek approval by sucking up to others, try not to offend at the cost of honest communication and believe they are right no matter what the circumstance.

As I was wrapping up this chapter I noticed that every time I would edit, I found it less and less funny until a *knuckleball* hit me in the gut. Of course I knew their quirks so well.

I am a member of each one of these tribes.

Oops.

My discovery that I was as much of a participant in these tribes as those I poked fun at gave my ego as well as my conscience a good kick in the behind. I may not be an avid tribal member at church, but I certainly can be one in my community and in society at large. I may use different tactics or scar people in different ways, but the fact remains that I can name numerous occasions when I have gossiped, was stubborn, acted like a sloth, marked my territory, didn't care about boundaries, didn't speak my mind, thought I was right no matter what and, worst of all, tried to shame people through manipulation.

A while ago I did some political mudslinging back and forth on social media with another person. By the time we finished we realized we were completely missing the point of the argument and came to a truce. Our promise to one another was that we would only think positive thoughts for the rest of the week when encountering other people – no judgments, no hate, no trying to prove a point.

I don't know about the guy on social media, but I couldn't go for a minute without something negative popping into my head. I'd tell myself to let go of the negativity and would then go back to being positive. Another couple minutes – BAM! – another negative thought. And this kept happening all week long! By the end of the week I was so frustrated with my pessimism I began to cry. Is this the way my instincts work? Am I really this vindictive?

In the most blatant way, I understood I needed to deprogram my way of thinking.

Tribes are everywhere – in work places, in locker rooms, in schools, in country clubs, on the floor of Congress – and churches are no different. I will be the first to admit that being sanctimonious is one of my biggest crosses to bear. I need to constantly remind myself I don't have all the right answers. In my own humble opinion, anyone who thinks they do have all the right answers takes away the one aspect of Christianity that makes it what it is – a mystery. There needs to be room for God to enter our minds.

I believe this term warrants a reminder:

Informal Social Control: Informal sanctions may include **shame, ridicule, sarcasm, criticism** and **disapproval**. In extreme cases sanctions may include **social discrimination** and **exclusion**.

Is the **Informal Social Control** standing in the way of your relationship with   other people in your life? With the members of your Church? Synagogue? Mosque? Community? God?

I found another definition for the word **Tribe** that I deem to be more suitable:

A group of people that is dependent upon each other for survival

I'm Wasted

I t's 10:30 on a Wednesday night and Charlie has been at church since 9:00 a.m. His regular office hours from 9:00-noon is busy with staff and people who drop by for pastoral guidance. The afternoon is more than likely spent reviewing his class lesson for Confirmation and studying up on readings for his sermon on Sunday. He meets with the Confirmation kids, if he has time he'll join the choir to rehearse, and afterward meets with the contemporary worship leadership team.

When he gets home he sits in his favorite recliner in our basement and simultaneously watches TV and decompresses by logging onto the Internet to check sports stats, or hops on one of the many sites selling anything that relates to one of his many hobbies. Within minutes his mind drifts into another world.

I ask him, "How was your day, honey?"

Whether it was filled with fires to be put out or just a regular work day I hear him say, "Hmm...Okay." There is no eye contact.

I'll go back to watching TV and Charlie continues his decompression. Fifteen minutes go by and he comes up to me and gives me a kiss on the cheek.

"I'm going to bed, sweetie...I'm wasted."

Since Charlie and I had been married for a few years before his call I was perplexed by his lack of communication once he began working full-time for a church. The reality was, to talk about the complexities of his work day he would need to relive it all over again. What he wanted from home life was relaxation from it.

I have come to recognize that in many ways a pastor has a lonely life and often, so does the pastor's wife or husband. Much of what goes on in a pastor's day is confidential. Some will share what stresses them with their colleagues but oftentimes not with their spouses. After ministering to people all day the last thing my husband wants to do is bring shop talk home with him.

I have interviewed many women who are married to pastors and asked them what is the most difficult part of being a pastor's wife.

I was alarmed by the answer. Every single woman said it hurt them to see how cruelly and maliciously some people treated their husbands. They mentioned some of the vicious remarks their husbands had to endure and frankly, I was appalled. Sometimes it trickles down into the pastor's family and causes much discord. Looking back at my college days it doesn't surprise me that half the PKs at my school rebelled against organized religion.

The rate of divorce among pastors has now matched the national rate and that is gravely unfortunate. Spouses often can't handle the amount of stress their loved one endures by serving a church. One pastor friend of mine was going through a divorce and to start a new life, he took a new call. In his exit interview the council asked him if he had any last words. In his kind and gentle manner he told them, "I'm glad the congregation treats other members who are going through a divorce better than they treat their pastor."

Another pastor once said to me, "Church life would be so much easier if it wasn't for all the religious people telling me what a heretic I am."

What is it about certain people that makes them feel they can say anything on their mind and not think it's going to affect their pastor both emotionally and spiritually? Do they believe that because a pastor has been "called" she or he can deflect words like a shield and they will simply bounce away? Are pastors perhaps holier than the rest of the congregation and therefore able to offer immediate forgiveness and not feel any pain?

My husband is private to a fault. Anything that is said between a parishioner and him is completely confidential. He will not confide in me with good news, bad news, or when he has been verbally abused. The only way I find out is through the Gossip Tribe.

There is a reason why there is pastor burn-out and many choose a different career in mid-life or perhaps even sooner. Pastors are one thing before anything else –they are *human*. They hurt and they grieve. They are called to teach and preach the gospels and to administer the sacraments. What often happens is they must constantly do damage control because people have their own agendas and can sometimes make it known to them in the most hurtful ways. Would a parishioner talk to their co-worker, spouse, or children in the same manner? If so, they would be fired for insubordination, or their loved ones would leave them, severely scarred.

The scars I see left on pastors are the weary eyes, the fatigue, the lines in their faces and the unseen bruises from people who have used them as their verbal punching bags.

I'm wasted. I hear that phrase from a lot.

The demanding hours and the function of being a spiritual and emotional guide can be exhausting for Charlie or any pastor. If you add the "shame factor" into the equation, I can understand how anyone who has been called to this profession would feel wasted.

Shame is a horrible emotion. Shame kills the soul. People will use it on pastors and their families for whatever purpose they feel will satisfy some deep, dark place within them. One person tried to shame me by telling me I will "need to testify on the last day" simply because I voted for a political candidate who I felt would do a better job at governing than the other. I didn't mince words with him. I told him he was presumptuous to appoint himself my Hell Sheriff and if he was trying to evangelize through condemnation he was only pissing me off.

Pastors' wives have written volumes of books in their heads, though for the most part they don't become published. When a pastor's wife sees two people across the room talking to one another but looking at her or her husband with disparaging eyes, she wants to write a book. When she and her husband have made plans together and their date is thwarted by what someone in the congregation thinks is a life-or-death situation, she wants to write a book. When her kids say and do normal things, misbehaving, and word gets around of the *horrors* they've perpetrated, she wants to write a book. Most of all she wants the world to know of the juggling it takes to work, raise kids, help keep her husband sane amid church politics and still manage to keep her own sanity intact. And then be introduced to people as The Pastor's Wife, with no name attached.

I hate to burst anyone's bubble, but guess what? Pastors' families are just as normal and dysfunctional as the rest of the world. We argue, we cuss (just drop in when the Packers are playing poorly and you'll know what I mean), and some of us imbibe alcoholic libations, smoke or overeat, sometimes in excess in order to deal with the modern-day Pharisees in our lives. We have our vices and we feel the same pain everyone else feels when dealing with them. None of us had children through Immaculate Conception and even when not attempting to procreate we try to find the time to remain intimate – if we're not wasted.

My husband and I are not perfect parents and our children are not perfect. I highly doubt any of them will become pastors. They're at a point in their lives where they are on their own spiritual journey. How that journey manifests itself is between them and their God. Through that process they may not end up believing in a manner that society judges to be proper Christian or religious belief; however, they have shown more love and mercy toward people than many who claim they are devout Christians. I'm very proud of them. We tried our best to teach them how to care for and love others, much in the way Jesus did. The rest is up to them.

I'm asking all of you out there to give your pastors and their families or your other religious leaders a break. Don't put any of us on a pedestal as we have never asked for it nor deserve it. By doing so, you will set yourselves up for disappointment.

Facing the Demons – Reprise

If you haven't figured it out by now, I'm not an outwardly religious person. Talking about God isn't my M.O. I feel uncomfortable praying out loud, even when it comes to saying grace at the table.

There are people in this world who with their entire heart and soul believe in God. Or Allah or Buddha or the Resurrection of Jesus or how the world operates in some metaphysical terms. For a long time, I would have given *anything* to be that sure of my faith. I would tell myself if I just tried a little harder, if I'd just repeat the Apostles' Creed enough times, if I just raised my hands to the sky when I sang praise songs, if I just...

It wasn't happening.

Why, when I was a child, could I believe in someone or something intangible and now have so many doubts, so many questions?

A few years back I went through a very dark time, a PTSD period, and I felt the proverbial rug pulled out from under me. I was in a stupor trying to deal with my past and at the same time I was pissed as hell. Charlie is very perceptive and pressed me with some questions.

"What or who is making you so angry?"

"That 'being' everyone calls God."

"Have you told God how angry you are?"

"No."

"Why not?"

"It's not polite," I said with heavy sarcasm.

He sat quietly for a moment and then asked me a weird question. "Do you trust me?"

I had no clue where he was going with this. I was peeved at his question. "Of course I trust you. What the hell does that have to do with my anger?"

He continued. "Do you trust me enough that you could say anything, no matter how much it would hurt me or would disappoint me and know that I would never leave you?"

Wow. I had to think about that one.

"Even if I said I hated you and told you that you were a son-of-a-bitch-douche-bag and thought you were the most disgusting person I knew?"

He laughed and said, "Yeah, even that."

I thought about it for a while more and evaluated this relationship I had with him: his kindness, his forgiveness, his unconditional love.

I finally said, "Yes...I trust that I could say anything and you would never leave me."

He was very sober and simply said, "Then how much more do you believe you can say anything to God, and God will never leave you? What have you got to lose?"

I thought about it for a moment, and then I went to get my coat.

"Where are you going?" he asked.

"I'm going to the gas station to pick up a pack of cigarettes. I won't be able to get through this without them."

So when I got back home, I built a fire outdoors, lit up one cigarette after another and for the second time in my life, I let God have it. By the time I was through I'd poured out all my hatred toward God and sobbed until my soul was empty. I also got so puking nauseous I didn't want to even look at another cigarette.

I mentioned this dialogue with God to someone who considers herself a believer and she just about flipped out that I would, as she put it, "go there." Go where? To a place where I had the audacity of confronting God in anger? That I wasn't honoring or respecting God in an appropriate way? The mere fact that I "went there" was evidence I believed in an Almighty Being. I had sobbed all the crap out of my soul and even my body responded by retching out anything else that was poisoning me emotionally.

As my soul had been emptied out of the rot, something else came in to fill it. Sometimes it was excruciating pain; sometimes I needed to tell myself it was okay for my soul to chill out; sometimes I felt something in my heart giving me comfort. As I began to slowly strengthen over the next few days I knew the tough healing work was still ahead of me. Again I had to go back to regular therapy with Jillian and pull out more of the repugnance.

Something very profound happened to me. I learned that many of the things that had occurred in my life that obstructed normal function were for the most part, a result of other people having junk and getting slammed with it. It wasn't just my depression, anxiety and PTSD I needed to deal with. I had to deal with everyone else's junk who lived both before me and with me.

With Jillian I began to see everyone's junk – my parents', my grandparents', my siblings', my children's, my first husband's, the grim-faced priest's at St. Stephen's, the snotty girl's who told lies about me to one of my high school boyfriends, they all have junk. And yes, even my very loving husband has junk. No one is immune to it. No one goes through life without pain or suffering or, *most of all*, skeletons in the closet. I'm not the only person with junk. I learned I am called as a human being to understand that and live my life according to that truth.

I had been programmed to think that there was one and only one way to be a believer, and it was what society deemed appropriate. Go to church. Obey the Ten Commandments. Give ten percent to charity. Don't swear. Behave in a normal, appropriate way in public. Don't say anything that might remotely offend anyone.

Hello-oh!!!!

This is Talia; the person one counselor asked if anyone had ever told her she was unconventional. Why then should my belief system be conventional?

Some people's spiritual M.O. is to get up early every morning, read scripture and go about their day using the inspired words to make everyone's day a little better. Mine is to go about my daily business and if I'm flipped the bird by someone in traffic, I need to say to myself, "Everyone Has Junk."

I have heard this statement from more people than I can count: "I'm very tolerant; I'm just not tolerant with the intolerant."

It's easy to tolerate people who feel the same way we do, but if they are intolerant to what is our own truth, then we can't stand them.

Some guy named Jesus, along with many other enlightened people told us to love and forgive our enemies.

Really? You've *got* to be kidding!

Nope, not kidding. In a most unconventional way I needed to grasp onto the fact that until I understood that all other people have junk and I loved and forgave them anyway, my junk will just keep coming back to haunt me. What I do to someone else I do to myself, whether it is inherently good or inherently bad.

I also threw out society's view that having mental illness made me less of a person and realized I could actually use my mental health struggles to empower the lives of others.

If I was born wired with mental illness perhaps I could better fight for the underdog. If I was so broken maybe I could identify with others who were broken as well. When I was cast aside because of the stigma of divorce, I could fully understand the sting for those who were treated as failures just because they were single parents. If society treated me unjustly for that divorce I could have empathy with someone who was wired to love someone of their own gender, facing many in a society that sneer at them. In the process of going through painful therapy I could understand just what hard work it is for people to overcome addictions.

It all goes back to the word Tribe: *A group of people who are dependent upon each other for survival.*

Some people's junk can be horrendous. As part of a functional tribe we don't condone the atrocities that are reprehensible nor do we condemn that person to eternal hell because frankly, no person on this earth is the Almighty Judge.

Sometimes a person needs a shoulder to cry on. Sometimes it means a call to the police. Sometimes it means being so frank with someone that it may compromise your relationship with him or her. And sometimes the best thing for that person is to let them go. Tribes are dependent on each other, not co-dependent.

So there is my epiphany. Everyone has junk. That is part of my belief system. I am called to love and forgive the junked-up people and wish them all good things in life. Every day I need to remind myself these thoughts:

To the people who lie, cheat and do anything to get what you want, I understand you were probably spoiled as a child.

I'm sorry you have junk.

To the people who blame everyone else for their problems, I understand that's probably what your abusive parent did.

I'm sorry you have junk.

To the people who betray others in their friendships, their marriages, their families, I understand you didn't have good examples of a relationship.

I'm sorry you have junk.

To the people who take away childhood innocence, I understand you were probably tortured and stripped of your innocence as well.

I'm sorry you have junk.

To the people who feel they have no spirit or try to break the spirit of everyone else, I understand how those who called themselves religious betrayed you or turned you off.

I'm sorry you have junk.

To the people who can't accept anything but perfection, I understand you could never live up to your family's expectations.

I'm sorry you have junk.

To the people who feel those who are mentally ill just need to suck it up, I understand you have never yourself gone through the depths of hell.

I'm sorry you have junk and I truly don't wish hell upon you.

And to God, whom I often curse, accuse, hate, feel betrayed by, can't figure out, I acknowledge that others and I fall short of perfection.

Thank you for enlightening me to a weird, unconventional belief system and understanding our junk.

If you're feeling the weight of the world on your shoulders or feel less than worthy, take a look at your personal Mode of Operation. Do you feel like a rat on a wheel sometimes, trying so hard to move forward but getting nowhere?

Analysis and therapy are wonderful tools. Talk it out, cry it out, yell it out, pray it out, whatever works for you. Discover for yourself the unique person you were created to be. It may not be enjoyable all the time. It may be quite painful. But I can pretty much guarantee one thing: you'll be getting rid of some junk.

Tallulah

Back in the 1980s when I was living in the Washington, D.C., area I was performing in the show *Funny Girl* at a place many of us in the cast referred to as "The Truck Stop Dinner Theatre." Semi-truckers literally gassed up their vehicles at the truck stop next door and would often spend the night in the motel that housed the theatre. The meager stage, green room and dressing area were located in the middle of nowhere, or so most people thought.

The National Security Agency (NSA) was only about two miles away with no signs designating the location of this covert organization in the 1980s. I knew the agency headquarters were there as I had applied to be a translator only six months earlier. Despite not being hired, I kept telling the cast they should keep their eyes open for anything suspicious. I told them the NSA had a file on me and anything I, or any people in my company did, was fair game for the agents to search, confiscate or question. I would throw in my Ukrainian/Russian accent every so often just to keep the cast amused and I enhanced this ruse by using my full legal name, Natalia. Everyone at the Truck Stop Dinner Theatre called me Natalia. Everyone except for a woman named Phyllis Goldblatt.

Phyllis was probably somewhere in her fifties but due to her diet of coffee and cigarettes she looked more as if she were on the north side of eighty. Her hair was dyed a weird red-orange, she wore dark blue eye shadow all the way to her eyebrows, her preferred fabric was animal print and her most famous quote was "lips and nails were meant to be red." She hated all the girls, loved all the boys and was never without a lipstick-stained cup of coffee and a cigarette burning from her long, red fingertips. She was a living caricature and if she disliked something, nothing short of vulgarity came out of her mouth. Phyllis had a permanent sneer on her face even when she smiled. The fact that she had an accent from some borough of New York only added to her shocking personality. She was also known to stretch the truth so a person never quite knew if what she said was real or fantasy. She was widowed, and we once asked her how her husband had died.

She gave us a deadpan look and said, "I killed him."

It was as good an answer as any.

One day before a performance, I was putting on my makeup where apparently Phyllis had been sitting before me. When she returned from the bathroom, I received her patented sneer. She lit up a cigarette and was looking for her coffee when she spotted her cup by me. Too lazy to get up she looked at me and said in her thick dialect, with disdain in her voice, "...Na...Na...Tallulah, or whatevah the fuck yo' name is, hand me my cawffee..."

The entire cast lost it, and from then on until the end of the run, everyone called me Tallulah.

About a dozen years later, I met up with a friend from *Funny Girl*, Franco, in Manhattan. He said, "Tallulah, I heard some news about Phyllis!"

Expecting something crazy, I exclaimed, "What? What is it?"

He took a puff from an imaginary cigarette and spoke with her expressionless baritone voice and a sneer on his face.

"Dead."

Oh, well. I'm sure she is amusing spirits somewhere.

About a year into Charlie's full-time call, a group of elderly people had a Scandinavian-style Christmas lunch. He and I were asked by someone if we could come up with some entertainment so we developed a skit. And so, Tallulah Goldblatt came into being.

Tallulah is third cousin on Talia's mother's side of the family who is Ukrainian and is Jewish on her father's side. She lives in Blattsborough, which is the sixth unknown borough of New York, squished in between

Queens and Brooklyn. The only building in Blattsborough is the funeral home, where she lives in an apartment above the parlor rent free by being the graveyard shift answering service and make-up artist (she thought Talia's living arrangements at a funeral home were ingenious!) Somewhere along the genealogical lines she and Phyllis are related and have an affinity for the same make-up and wardrobe as well as the shockingly red hair. That's about all they have in common. Tallulah never stops smiling and is always asking people to be her new best friend. Somehow every time she makes an appearance we find out more and more things about her:

Tallulah has been married five times to customers of the "parlor" after consoling the bereaved widowers. She has also been widowed five times herself, as each husband has never lived through a full year of marriage with her. They couldn't keep up with her exuberance.

Tallulah always tries to put the limelight on other people to make them feel important and loved. She would, however, accept the lime-light just to be a contestant on the TV reality show, *Dancing with the Stars*. She believes if everyone dressed and danced the way they do on the program, the United Nations would have a permanent peace solution.

Tallulah thinks a "potluck" might be something illegal. She hasn't checked to see if legalizing marijuana was on the latest ballot in Minnesota so she's not taking any chances of going to one there.

Tallulah is ordained as the Very Left Rectoress of Perpetual Serenity and Eternal Lifesprings Church and Gluten-Free Brewery and received her ordination online. This allows her to perform impulsive wedding ceremonies and funerals, as she doesn't believe one should take the "fun" out of funeral.

Tallulah has also given a sermon at Charlie's church. When people know she is in town, worship attendance doubles.

I usually go to Manhattan once a year to rejuvenate my spirit, and one time I brought Tallulah with me. I was scheduled to stay at Franco's and his partner Kevin's condo. Tallulah appeared out of the ladies room at La Guardia Airport in New York in a leopard halter top, black sequined leggings, green eye shadow up to her eyebrows, a red-orange wig and of course, red lips and nails. She hailed a cab to the city (in which she and the cabbie had a wonderful conversation), and arrived at Franco and Kevin's place. She walked into the lobby where the doorman sat. He gave her a suspicious look and asked her who she was visiting. He rang up Franco and Kevin and skeptically announced Tallulah had arrived. He received the okay to send her up.

Upon arriving on the sixth floor she was chatting away talking to herself, trying to find the correct apartment, loud enough for everyone on the floor to hear her. Doors began to open. Franco finally opened his door and immediately Tallulah threw her arms around him as neighbors looked on warily. He was speechless. He had never seen her in person, only in pictures. Kevin's first thought was that Tallulah was some sort of drag queen. They asked her where Talia was and out came her story, Blattsborough accent and all, hardly taking a pause to breathe:

"omyGOSH OMYgosh, I have to tell you about my poor, dear cousin Talia who, unfortunately, not because she didn't brush or floss her teeth, as I hope you all don't think she has a problem keeping up with her hygiene, had to have two of her back teeth YANKED out a couple years ago, and once THAT happened, there were these bones chips that kept POKING out so on several occasions she had to go and have the oral surgeon G-R-I-N-D those little suckers, so now that all THAT is healed, she went to see the surgeon, the oral one, to replace those teeth and he says, sure, we can do that, and she says, what's gonna happen?, and he says, well, there's one area where your bone disintegrated because it wasn't being used and we'll inject it with human cadaver bone, and she says WHAT????? and he says, yes, it comes from people who donate their organs after death, which I must say, is a sweet way to leave a legacy, but for HER having cadaver bones in her mouth was a bit iffy, so I reassured her, since I do work at the "parlor," she will in no way be at risk of formaldehyde poisoning since they take the bone BEFORE I primp them up for the viewing, so she finally agrees, and THEN he tells her that the roots of the implants will be made out of titanium, which sounds to me like foreign matter developed

*by NASA, but she gets the implants anyway, so we're just walking around
the airport to fly out here, minding our own business when we pass by a
TSA metal detector rod and everywhere lights are flashing, the danger
level turns to code red and an army of SWAT men, who I might add were
quite handsome, take her into a private room while I'm left standing wondering what they'll do to her, and in a few minutes the men come out of
the room laughing about the titanium rods in her head while everyone in
the airport is still under tables making cell phone calls to loved ones, and
frankly, I'm surprised it hasn't been on the news, for heaven's sakes, what
are they reporting on these days?, so she's home recovering from her titanium debacle and THANK GOODNESS for Vicodin and ice cold chocolate
ice cream, and the next time you see her, make sure you're not carrying
any magnets or you may become uncomfortably close to her, so now after
all this excitement I REALLY need to use your little girl's room, K? K."*

The guys were beside themselves laughing. After a significant time
in the bathroom, the long orange hair and makeup were gone and surprisingly, Talia was now in their living room.

Later in the evening Kevin said, "I think we need Tallulah to come
with us to the karaoke bar this week. Everyone will love her!"

A few nights later, from midnight to 4:00 a.m., Tallulah spread
her charm at a gay karaoke bar. Not only was she a hit at singing, she
became quite popular, as everyone in the bar had a chance to talk with
her, received a huge bear hug and became her new best friend. On her
way out the owner gave her his business card to call him when she was
in town again to schedule her for an appearance.

Tallulah may be a character I made up with certain traits like Phyllis
Goldblatt's, but she is also a very big part of me.

There are days when my spirit feels as if it's shriveling away living
a society that is so uptight about certain rules of behavior. I absolutely
hate hearing antiquated phrases such as "that's not ladylike" or "don't
embarrass yourself."

Screw it. By throwing on a wig, wearing flamboyant clothes, using
make-up that looks absolutely absurd, and displaying a personality

different from who I am on an everyday basis, I feel a sense of liberation. I'd perform her more often if she wasn't so exhausting.

I'm pretty lucky to have a third cousin like Tallulah. When I'm feeling down and can't seem to shake it off, she is always close by to remind me that life is filled with abundant, brazen joy, and the only BFFs you don't have are the ones you haven't met yet.

The Home

I'm sitting in the chapel of the neighborhood senior living facility. The annual Service of Remembrance is taking place to honor those who have died the past year who lived on this very large campus. The chaplain calls out a name and family members of the deceased are there to receive a cross with their loved one's name on it. It's a beautiful gesture of looking back on a person's life and the hopes or beliefs we all have that they are at peace and that we'll be reunited with them someday.

The atmosphere is reverent and calm. A family suddenly appears in the chapel, late for the service and with them is an elderly woman I recognize, one who lives in one of the facility's memory units – a cozy eight bedroom home for people who are losing their cognition. They all find seats in the back. The chaplain calls out a name and a man stands up and walks to receive the cross. All of a sudden the silence is broken.

"Holy SHIT! I didn't know he died!!"

The elderly woman who came in late is flabbergasted with this news while every other person is doing their best to stifle the inevitable hilarity of the situation by coughing, snorting, and some just can't help themselves and break out into full laughter.

Ah yes, The Home. The campus in our picturesque lake community is a place where seniors reside, all the way from independent living to nursing care. I like calling it The Home because that's truly what it is. For most people, it's the last place they will live.

Many people cringe when they are asked to go visit someone or volunteer in a nursing home. More than likely it's a knee-jerk response because the reality is that some of us will in fact live in a nursing home and the thought of it seems unpleasant for those still young and healthy. What many people never get to see is the humor, camaraderie, love and just plain peculiarity of people who live and work at a nursing facility.

I was looking for a part-time job and decided to see what employment might be open at The Home. I had worked in a long-term care facility during the summers of my college years in the activity department and I enjoyed it, so I went on the website of this senior living facility and under employment here is what I found:

Wanted: Half-time person for recreation therapy. Must have music skills. Previous experience desired.

I found it freakishly coincidental.

I applied and was hired. I would be working in the long-term care area of the facility, providing music and recreation therapy.

People who work outside of recreation therapy, as well as the residents, more than likely think we spend our day simply having fun with everyone. We do, but our fun time is short-lived in an eight-hour day. Perhaps twenty percent of our day is consumed with fun activities; about eighty percent is devoted to dealing with administrative details and damage control that inevitably come up in a building that houses up to one hundred people. On my slowest day, my pedometer clocked four miles. On my busiest day, nine. The most important qualification is cheerfulness, even when you're feeling miserable. No resident wants to hear of your woes or discomfort. They have enough of their own.

During one of my first weeks working there, I added a few days of work to my schedule to cover for a vacationing colleague. I was still fairly new to the job and I had worked six days in a row so I was dog-tired, to say the least.

The last activity of the day was "musical memories" in the day room of the area that housed people with the lowest cognition. I gathered a group of residents to sit by me and started singing old folk songs and familiar hymns.

I had no idea I was going to have competition.

In the day room was Lois, "The Rapper." She spoke to herself a lot. Remarkably, she did so in four-line stanzas that rhymed. Example:

And now I know
There was a boy
He wants to go
And get his toy

I began the activity by playing and singing an easy hymn with the guitar. While I sang, Lois kept rapping, and with each new piece I played she rapped louder. I thought, perhaps, if I played a familiar hymn, she might be persuaded to sing along. It ended up sounding something like this:

"Amazing grace..."
    "And now I know..."
"How sweet the sound..."
    "I hear a song..."
"That saved a wretch..."
    "You need to go..."
"Like me..."
    "Would somebody tell her TO SHUT UUUUPPP??!!"

I had the longest, most tiring work week of my life, was punch-drunk with laughter and I couldn't collect myself. She gave me this odd look and said, "Well. What the hell are you waiting for, dammit?! Are you going to sing or not?! Don't just sit there!"

Lois allowed me to continue. One woman, Emily, sat with her eyes closed as I started "Home on the Range." She never spoke with anyone or responded when someone asked her a question. When the song came to the refrain she opened her eyes and in full voice belted out,

"HOME, HOME ON THE RANGE WHERE THE DEER AND THE ANTELOPE PLAY! WHERE SELDOM IS HEARD A DISCOURAGING WORD AND THE SKIES ARE NOT CLOUDY ALL DAY!"

She finished singing and simply continued sitting with a very dry look on her face as if singing out loud was an everyday occurrence.

The next song was Clementine. I began singing the verse:

"In a cavern, in a canyon, excavating for a mine,
Lived a miner, forty-niner and his daughter, Clementine."
*"HOME, HOME ON THE RANGE WHERE THE DEER AND THE
ANTELOPE PLAY! WHERE SELDOM IS HEARD A DISCOURAGING
WORD AND THE SKIES ARE NOT CLOUDY ALL DAY!"*

Apparently Emily was ready to sing the refrain to "Home on the Range" for every song that day. There was no way to stop her. Nor did we try.

❉

Besides singing with the guitar in the evening before residents went to bed, my other favorite activity was The Home Choir.

One resident, Ethel, had come down with a stroke years before and the right side of her body was paralyzed. She couldn't speak anymore, but when participating in choir she could match the pitches and mouth the words. We were approaching the Christmas holidays and wanted to knock the socks off everyone attending the Christmas service. On one piece Ethel held the tambourine in her left hand, keeping the beat. We were a hit.

After the service the choir and I went into the back conference room to have coffee. Ethel and her daughter both came up to me with tears of gratitude streaming down their faces. Ethel's daughter said, "Talia, my mom has never done anything like this since her stroke. I can't thank you enough." Ethel was nodding her head up and down, still speechless and crying, but her communication to me was apparent. She had spent decades as a church organist and since her stroke was unable to do anything musically except play the little keyboard that sat in her room with her left hand.

We decided we were so good we'd go on the road. So we did, over to the church my husband serves. In between services The Home Choir gave a thirty-minute concert. When we ended it with our gospel style, "Go Tell It on the Mountain," there wasn't a person left sitting.

Applause, whistles, catcalls, tears, you name it. The choir and I found out something: you're never too old to inspire others.

※

I met my match with a woman named Miriam. Someone else in my department was assigned to her initial interview and came back from it perplexed by her answers and possibly, a bit unnerved by her personality. I took a moment to review Miriam's answers on the interview sheet. When I had a break in time, I stopped by her room.

"Hi Miriam, my name is Talia. I work in recreation therapy."

"Really," she replied. "Have you come to check up on the latest inmate here?

"As a matter of fact, I have. I wanted to find out if you preferred a striped uniform or the latest glow-in-the-dark orange."

She hesitated for a moment. "I like you. You have chutzpah."

"Gotta have chutzpah to keep up with someone like you." She gave me a big smile.

"So," I continued, "you aren't interested in any of the spiritual programs here?"

"Nope," she said firmly. "I prefer imagining myself in the middle of the California redwoods and to connect with the spiritual world that way."

"I've never tried that," I responded.

"Well, maybe you should. You won't be tempted to fall asleep during a sermon."

"Well, maybe I will."

I moved onto a new subject.

"I understand you enjoy music. What type of music do you enjoy the most?"

"Well, none of that crap they play on Christian radio around here."

"You're talking about Jeezak?" I asked.

"What the hell is Jeezak?"

"It's a combination of Jesus songs and Muzak."

She gave a hearty laugh. "You *are* a salty one."

"I do my best," I responded. "I understand you play the cello."

"Yes, I did," Miriam said, "but that was years ago."

"I'm scheduled to play piano during coffee hour next week. Would you like to come?"

Miriam smirked. "Depends – will it be Jeezak?"

"Nope. I dislike Jeezak myself. How about some standard classical piano?"

"Well, I might be convinced to come if it's classical."

The next week I went to her room and brought her to the dining room for coffee hour. I played Mozart, Chopin, Beethoven, Debussy, and she sat with her eyes closed the entire time. After the coffee hour I was ready to bring her back to her room.

"Please don't stop," Miriam asked. "It's so nice to hear live classical music again."

I could spare the time, and for an extra forty-five minutes I played, just the two of us enjoying ourselves with a common bond of classical music.

The following Sunday I knocked on Miriam's door shortly before worship was to begin.

She looked at me and frowned. "I told you, I don't go to church."

"I'm not bringing you there. I don't work today. I came today to join you in the California redwoods."

❉❂❉

My most precious moment was with a woman named Mabel. She was ninety-seven years old and every resident loved and respected her. Mabel came down with a severe case of pneumonia and refused to be admitted into a hospital. Despite feeling so miserable, she phoned her family and asked them to come over one afternoon and to also bring her great-grandchildren. Mabel sat in her rocking chair, two toddlers climbing on and off of her lap and by 4:00 in the afternoon the family left. I was working until 5:00 that day and just as I was leaving the building I felt a strong urge to turn around and stop by her room to see how she was doing. She didn't look at all well. I asked her if I could get her anything and she said some soup would be nice. The dietary staff brought her a bowl and put it on her bed tray.

Mabel was so weak she couldn't even feed herself. I was ready to help her eat when she looked at me and asked, "Aren't you supposed to be gone by now?"

I smiled and said, "I'd just be going home to an empty house."

Her eyes began to glisten with tears. "Oh dear, you're my angel."

"No, Mabel, I'm far from being an angel. I just want you to be comfortable."

"No, you're my angel" she kept insisting.

"You've just never noticed the devil's horns underneath my hair," I teased. Mabel was able to muster up a smile.

After eating about half a bowlful she became restless. Her clothes were bothering her. She kept pulling at them. Finally she said, "Talia, please help me. My clothes are burning me."

I knew her life would be short as I had seen others who were dying pulling away at their clothes as if they literally wanted to take their skin off their body as if to set their spirit free.

I tried to offer her some assistance by helping her take off her sweater. She was still very uncomfortable. "Help me," she pleaded.

I decided it was time to call for a nurse to administer something to alleviate her discomfort. A tranquilizer was given to her as the nurse helped her swallow it down with applesauce. She held onto my hand so tightly my fingers were turning blue.

"You shouldn't be here Talia, your husband needs you at home," she said.

"My husband is just fine. You know I'm only staying with you in case the nurse leaves behind some doped-up applesauce."

Mabel giggled. She looked at me one more time and again said, "You're my angel." She kept repeating it until the tranquilizer kicked in.

I had never been this close to death. I sat very quietly with her until her grasp on my hand relaxed.

"Are you feeling better?" I asked her.

"So much better," she said. At this point there was nothing more I could do. "Mabel, I'm going to let you go to sleep. You'll be leaving us soon so I'll kiss you good-bye. If you're still with us in the morning I'll sing to you."

Her eyes began to close. "God be with you..."

The next morning Mabel was unconscious. I sang a few short songs to her, noticing her breathing was irregular. I left the room and when the nursing assistant went in five minutes later, Mabel was gone.

The Home is a good place to respect the process of death. Some die in their sleep, some see angels, some are up and about one day and are gone the next. They've come to a place in their lives where they can spend the day how they wish and when it's time to let go, they let go.

Miriam, Ethel, Lois and Emily have left and have joined Mabel. Working at The Home isn't just a job. It's a calling for someone who wants to use their spiritual gift of conversation. It's also a place that helps remind you that up until the moment someone takes their last breath, they have something wonderful to offer the world.

Pennies from Heaven

In the late winter of 2007 my dad was eighty-three years old. On more than one occasion my brothers and I tried to convince him to sell his house to make his life easier. He would become infuriated and say, "Selling this house would be like putting one foot in the grave!" He was fiercely independent and sometimes a stubborn man – not the kind who becomes a curmudgeon, but he knew what he wanted and at his age no one was going to tell him what to do.

Hardly a winter goes by in Minnesota without the state getting blessed by two-foot snow drifts. My brothers lived near my dad and always made it a point to head over to his place to take on the physical labor of moving the snow, which he refused to delegate to a younger person in the neighborhood who was looking to make a few bucks. One Sunday morning, well before my brothers got to his house, he'd already been out with heavy boots up to his knees, a thick winter coat and the patented head gear with ear flaps that depicts the Northland winter weather so stereotypically. He was making a path with his snow shovel inch by inch to the garage to remove that one important piece of equipment every Minnesotan cherishes – the mighty snow blower.

He and my brothers spent the entire morning clearing the steps, the sidewalk, the driveway and the huge mound of snow the city plow left behind along the entryway to the sidewalk. They finished their enormous task and went inside the house. The work exhausted my dad and both my brothers knew it. My oldest brother's temperament got the best of him.

"Dad, you really need to sell this house. You're too old to be doing this type of work!"

"I don't want to sell the house."

"Dad, you're exhausted! Sell the damn house!"

"I don't want to sell the house."

"Someday you're going to be outside shoveling snow and you'll die of a heart attack!"

"That's not so bad. Dying quickly would be nice."

"Geez, Dad, *sell the house!*"

"I don't want to sell the house."

Later that afternoon my oldest brother called me.

"Talia, you've *got* to tell Dad to sell his house."

"Why don't you tell him?"

"I did tell him!"

"What did he say?"

"I don't want to sell the house!"

I took a deep breath. Finally I sighed and said, "I'll see what I can do."

I decided I would take a trip into town the next day and try to worm my way into the discussion of putting the house up on the market. As I was thinking about my approach my phone rang. The caller ID showed it was my dad. I took a moment to organize my arsenal of reasoning and picked up the phone.

"Hello..."

"Hi, Talia..."

"Hiya, Pop..."

"Say, I've got something to ask you." At this point I was ready to hear about the discussion he'd had with my brother. "Have you ever heard of 'pennies from heaven'?"

"Uh...what...?" I was dumbfounded.

He was more insistent. "Have you ever heard of 'pennies from heaven'?"

Okay Talia, he has something obscure on his mind; I don't know where this is going; just humor him.

"Well, I know there's a song written by that name. I also think it's a good luck superstition; if you find a penny by accident, you look at the date and you remember something good that happened that year. Why do you ask?"

At this point my dad was beside himself. "I must have gone up and down the stairs a dozen times today and I know for a fact I didn't have any change in my pocket. Something was on my mind all day and I was about to call you when on the floor lay a bright, shiny penny in the sunlight."

"Well, you must have missed it the other times you went by."

Wrong answer. My dad's eyesight was so good he could pick out a mosquito from a wall of gnats.

"Listen, if I said it wasn't there before I was going to call you, it wasn't there!"

"Well, what year was it from," I asked.

"This year. 2007."

"So, just think of it as something good happening to you this year."

"Yeah..." My dad drifted off somewhere distant.

I continued. "By the way, I'm going to be in town tomorrow. I'll stop by."

"Sounds good. See you then." *Click.*

That was unusual. Once we were on the phone, we could easily talk for up to an hour.

The next day I came into his house and he was sitting in his favorite chair looking quite pensive.

"Hiya, Pop!"

My dad drew his brows together, contemplating. Without even a hello from him he said, "Talia...I think it's time to sell the house."

Silence.

I was surprised to hear this from him. Finally I asked, "What made you decide this?"

He gave me a serious look.

"Yesterday after clearing the snow I sat down in this chair and it took me two hours to get enough strength to go into the kitchen to make myself something to eat. Once I ate, I felt fine but I kept thinking I shouldn't be doing this kind of work anymore." He paused and stared at me. "And then, I found a penny from heaven."

He kept staring, knowing I would understand the penny he found was significant to him.

I sat on his footstool and looked him square in the eyes. "Are you sure?"

"I'm sure."

"Okay then, let's get the ball rolling."

Three months later his house was sold and he moved into his two-bedroom senior living apartment. No grass to cut, no gutters to clean and no two-foot snow drifts to forge through. A few months into his new place he was known by everyone in the building, as his charm was difficult to resist. By the time winter came again he said, "I should have sold the house years ago."

After the move my dad and I spent a lot of time together. Since my kids were grown and out of the house I ended up doing a lot of freelancing in the Twin Cities. If I was there for consecutive days, I'd bring an overnight bag and sleep in his second bedroom, the old twin bed I had slept in all my childhood waiting for me. We got back in the routine of long breakfasts over coffee. An entire generation had passed and yet I felt nothing had changed except for a few extra years of wisdom.

2010 was a tough year for my dad. He had a day surgery procedure for his prostate, both of his eyes were operated on for cataracts, and there were signs of glaucoma. In the late fall, two of his friends from St. Stephen's had died, one of them being the very first Ukrainian he met when moving to St. Paul. The visitations and funerals were only days apart from each other and as I drove him back home from the second visitation we were both very quiet. Something was going on in both our minds and neither of us wanted to say anything out loud. I dropped him off, we said our good-byes and I love yous and I continued to drive the thirty-five minutes back to my small town. While I waited for a traffic light to change I knew that at some point my brothers and I would be dealing with my dad's funeral. All of a sudden something blurted out of my mouth...

"...June 2011..."

I was so stunned by the involuntary outburst the person behind me had to honk to get me to drive on the green light.

After the New Year of 2011 I noticed little things about my dad. His daily walks were shorter, his balance was off and he tired easily. In mid-May he was having trouble sleeping and had constant nausea. Daily he was feeling worse.

I called him to say I was going to stop by on my way to my college class reunion. He was waiting outside his door in the hallway when I got off the elevator and even from a long distance I could see him looking gaunt and frail. I came inside his apartment and without saying a word to each other we simply started hugging and crying. It was June 3, 2011. I walked him over to the couch and we continued with our tears until I felt I could speak.

"This is your time, isn't it?"

"Yep."

Yep. What more can anyone say?

"I don't have to go to my reunion. If you're not feeling well, I'll drive home and pack a suitcase and stay with you."

My dad wasn't going to have any of that type of nonsense. "No, you go. I'm fine for now and I just want to be alone for the time being."

Of course I had to go. His greatest pride was that his three children had all graduated from college. For me to be back on campus was a sign of victory for him.

When I arrived for the reunion lunch I met up with someone I didn't get to know very well when we were students, but I always admired him. He had been named bishop of one of the areas in Minnesota and I went to congratulate him.

"So, how have you been, Talia?"

"*Waaaaaaaahhhh!!!!!*" I'm slobbering all over this poor guy and without even asking a question, he just held me until my tears subsided. "My dad is dying."

I'd finally said it out loud. The first man I had ever loved in my life was going to leave me.

I kept up the daily calls. One evening he said, "I really feel awful. I need help." Without hesitating, I left work, packed up a few things and went to his apartment. I called his doctor the next morning describing his symptoms and he suggested I take my dad to the emergency room. I packed a small bag for him with all his medical information in a large envelope and he made one last stop to his closet to open up a metal suitcase. He pulled out his Advanced Directive, which stated he wanted only palliative care, simply medication and attention to his needs that would keep the rest of his life comfortable for him. He gave it to me and I tucked it safely in my purse. Just as we were leaving he slowly took one last look at the apartment. He was so weak I had to carry his light bag and hold his hand all the way to the car.

While he was lying in the ER a lot of blood was drawn and the whole time my dad just lay in bed quietly with his eyes closed most of the time. When the attending doctor told him his kidneys were failing and suggested medication and dialysis he motioned to me. I knew he wanted his Advanced Directive given to the doctor. As the doctor read it, he said, "You know, we can do something to keep you feeling better for a while."

My dad shook his head. "Listen, Doctor, you could do something and I could live six more months or maybe a year, but what kind of living would I have? I've lived a good life, I've made my peace with everyone and I know it's my time. I'm ready to go." The next day he was transferred to a hospice house to live out the rest of his life.

During the years after my mom had died, I wondered just how difficult it would be to see my dad go. I had my mom around for less than fifteen years; I had my dad for more than fifty. In the back of my mind I wondered if I would feel the sort of trauma I felt after my mom's death. I always thought it would be even harder to let go of him.

It wasn't. The reason?
We talked about it.

All of us had time to talk to our dad, tell him how much we loved him and listen to what he wanted for his funeral. My brothers and I took an afternoon to discuss the division of tasks, pulled pictures together, we cried when we felt like it, and the only way I can describe our experience was that we were privileged. Odd as it may sound, watching the process of him dying was a holy experience for me.

One day I sat with him while he was in some other world. I didn't want to speak out loud to disturb him, so I spoke to him in my mind in Ukrainian, the language he and my mother had taught me. I told him all of us in the family were so grateful to have him as a father and he was such a great dad. All of a sudden his eyes widened. He left whatever world he had been in and looked at me, lucid as ever.

"Did you hear what I was thinking?" I asked him.

He nodded, and astonished, told me word for word what I'd said to him in my mind.

I made the difficult decision to resign from my job at The Home. I so loved my work there yet I knew every day I could have to spend with him would be a gift for us both. My brothers and daughter all offered for me to stay with them so I wouldn't have to be alone in his apartment. I graciously declined as being among my dad's belongings, sleeping in the bed he had for sixty years, using the dishes I grew up with made me feel as if I was in a constant embrace by him.

One beautiful evening in July I ventured outside his apartment building. I was sipping a cocktail I'd made for myself, sitting on the curb of the parking lot. My attention was diverted to the blacktop where an old penny sat in the dirt. I picked it up and the year stamped on it was 1974, the year my mom died. A bittersweet feeling consumed me and I knew I needed to share the coin with my dad.

The next day I walked into his room and sat by his bed. I gave him an impish smile.

"Dad, I got a penny from heaven yesterday."

He gazed at me as I pressed the coin in his hand. He looked at it and saw the date. "Don't you see, Dad? It's the year Mama died."

He must have looked at it a good minute before speaking. Very softly he said, "Put it in my address book. At the visitation put it in the breast pocket of my suit coat." He then gave me a smile that lit up the room.

Towards the end of July, Dad was having a rough day. It was the sixtieth anniversary of his marriage to my mom. He was pulling at his clothes, agitated and pushing people away. I knew it was just a matter of a short time, maybe a few days before he'd leave us. It was getting late in the evening and I needed to leave so the nursing staff could take care of his bed-time routine. I kissed him good-bye and as I was walking out the door I gave one last glance toward him. He was lucid again, and looked at me with the deepest love I had ever seen in his eyes, and he gently waved. I knew in my heart it was his final good-bye.

From that point on Dad remained unconscious. It was August and by this time my daughter and I had cleaned out his apartment, so I drove to her place to spend the night. At one point in my drive I had this intense craving for M & Ms. I turned off the road, went into a convenience store and bought a package. When I received my change back, one bright 2011 penny sat in my hand.

I hurried to my daughter's apartment, picked her up and we drove straight to see my dad.

As I walked into his room I could feel the aura of another world. I lay right next to him and whispered in his ear:

"Dad, I got your penny from heaven today. I love you, I'll miss you, and it's time for you to go. You promised me you'd come and visit in my dreams. I'll be waiting."

My dad died the next morning.

At the visitation, two pennies were lovingly placed in his jacket pocket.

Two weeks later my daughter and I participated in a walk to raise money for breast cancer. After that weekend both my mom and dad came to see me in a dream, just as they were in the picture that sits on my desk, young and happy. My mom was whooping and hollering, congratulating me on my success for walking three straight days in a row.

My dad said nothing; he simply gave me his famous shit-eating grin. I slowly woke up with a huge smile on my face and for the first time ever since my mom died I'd had a dream about her that didn't haunt me. It was as if they were telling me they were exactly where they were supposed to be and didn't have a care in the world.

For about a year after my dad died I picked up many stray pennies lying on the ground. Most times I didn't think about them; I'd just slip them into a pocket and go about my business. Several times I experienced a strong impulse to look specifically at the date. Every single one I'd felt drawn to look at had been stamped 2011.

Precognition, Visions and Dreams

When I mention to people I have precognition, have seen a vision of a dead person and those who have died visit me in my dreams I generally receive a weird look where eyes are doubtful and a tenuous smile appears.

Vocal response: "...o...kay..."

It's easy for people to watch movies and TV shows that bring in psychic phenomena, but hearing someone talk about it happening in real life tends to give them the willies.

My introduction to precognition began when I was about thirteen and for a long time with insignificant things, and only sporadically. Before putting my key in the door of our house I would sense no one was home when I expected someone to be there. At card games I would know which card everyone was going to throw on the table. At times I could predict exactly what a person was going to say, especially when they wanted to change the subject. My sense is, when a person is first faced with precognition, if it's insignificant, it's handled without fear.

Precognition has developed as I have matured. Sometimes I will feel completely out of sorts with nothing to blame circumstantially for my anxiety, only to find out soon afterward that something tragic has happened to someone I know. I knew full well something significant would occur to my dad in June, 2011, when I burst that date out of my mouth six months earlier.

I also have the good karma on occasion. Wanting to find some additional antique dinner glasses matching those I had, I drove by a thrift store, had an impelling urge to stop the car, went in, and walked right to where I found six perfectly matched glasses. I can also find a parking spot in a crowded lot, either when I'm driving or when someone else is.

I owe my precognition to the DNA of my father's family, the Makovets'kys. My dad had dreams and precognitions regularly. Several of his uncles did as well. One of them won a two-million-peso lottery while living in Argentina by picking out a number he kept dreaming about.

Another uncle of his dreamt his brother died. The telephone hadn't quite made it to people's homes in Eastern Europe in the 1930s, so word of his brother's death would have arrived too late by mail for this uncle to attend the funeral. When he woke up from his dream he caught the first train to his home village and arrived that afternoon. The family was a bit startled to see him. He told them he dreamt about the death of his brother. "Ah, yes, of course..." they said, nodding their heads. "Nothing weird about that."

So what's the verdict here? Crazy or not crazy?

I do believe a person has to be somewhat peculiar, for wont of a better word, to have incidents like these happen to them. I also think a person has to *believe* that these events can occur and bear some sort of meaning.

It's kind of like going to an acupuncturist. If you go with reservations and can't stand the thought of scores of needles entering your body, acupuncture is not going to give you much relief. If you go with an open mind and needles don't bother you, it will relieve pain, anxiety, even the cravings of certain addictions. It certainly has worked for me regarding my physical and emotional health, and it hasn't for those I know who are skeptical.

When my dad's mother knew she was dying he asked her if it was possible to let him know in some way how she was, where she was, anything to know she was okay after she died. She promised him that if it was possible, she would. A few weeks after her death, she came to him in a dream.

My dad asked her, "What is it like, the other side?"

"More wonderful than you can imagine," she replied. He said she was glowing and more vital than he had ever seen her in his life.

When my dad was in hospice I said to him, "You know, your mother came to you at your request. I would like the same kind of visit. Also, please visit your granddaughter if you can. I know it would make Irina feel better."

He just grinned and nodded. Going through the process of his death was so difficult for her, even as an adult of twenty-five. I had never seen a grandparent and grandchild so close.

A day after my dream with him and my mom, my daughter called me and exclaimed, "Mom, I've *got* to tell you about a dream I had this morning about *Dido!*" (Ukrainian for Grandpa)

"You tell me yours first and then I'll tell you mine." Apparently someone was making house calls during the early morning hours of sleep.

About fifteen years ago, shortly after I started medication and therapy, I noticed my precognition coming back after a long hiatus. My instincts were telling me that I was healing from my trauma, because the more I kept stuffing my emotion, the less precognition I had. Jillian found it fascinating that I connected the two.

I was curious what a theologian would have to say about my prophetic episodes and thought it might be best to get an opinion from someone who didn't know me.

I decided to attend worship one Sunday at a mega-church I'd visited a few times. After the service I asked the pastor if I could have a word with him. I started out explaining how I experienced this "sixth sense" infrequently. He cut me off quickly and gave me a very strange look. He then proceeded to tell me I should watch out because it sounded as if Satan was working his way into my life. And then he walked away.

I stood there with my mouth open and couldn't utter a word. I was astonished by his presumption. Here I was looking for guidance and someone who didn't know me assumed Satan and I were hooking up somehow, not even taking the time to find out more about me or what was going on during my precognitions.

It's no wonder people who experience the paranormal are reticent to talk about it. There are skeptics who tell you it's all inside your head, religious leaders who say watch out – Satan is following you – and others who will argue that if you don't have scientific proof then it doesn't mean a thing.

Well then, call me crazy. My precognitions, visions and dreams are something I can hold onto when it's difficult to grasp the concept that Jesus was physically resurrected from the dead, or that Mary became pregnant through Immaculate Conception, or that God really spoke to Abraham, or Job or Moses. Something is happening out there that speaks to me through this absurd spiritual gift. When I dream of those I love who have died talking to me, happy, radiant, filled with an energy I've never experienced with them before, I can say this much: another world outside of the one we live in is *very* real to me.

Don't ask me to buy a winning lottery ticket for you, or predict who is going to win the Academy Award for Best Director. That stuff happened to my dad. He actually came out ahead about twenty-five bucks the handful of times he scratched his tickets, every single one of them winning. But ask me if I believe in an unseen, unscientific, unproved dimension and I'll say, "Ah, yes, of course...nothing weird about that."

The Next Chapter

Charlie and I live in a Mayberry kind of place. Every day at noon and at 6:00 p.m. a whistle blows signaling it's time to eat. I'm always bumping into someone I know, or several people for that matter, when I go shopping for groceries at the supermarket or stopping in at the coffee bar. The local convenience store is equipped with everything you need for optimum living in our lake community –gas, groceries, gyros and gill-bait. The auto repair shop actually gives a realistic estimate for repairs without pointing out a half dozen other things they can do with your car just to rake in money off of the ignorant who know nothing about the ins and outs of automobiles.

Communities, churches, families, they share the same things: the odd or bigoted relative you'd just as soon not have to deal with as well as a bond you learn to strengthen and accept. You have your spats. The most vehement combatants will either hold a grudge for life or agree to disagree. Most people in my community choose the latter.

Yet in small towns and small churches there are also treasures. It can drive me crazy when a person chooses to overstep boundaries, telling me or my husband what we "should" do, however, when I step back and take a deep breath I know that for the most part people are good-hearted and mean well.

As long as my husband and I have been part of this community we have received wonderful treasures from other people. The standard Minnesota "hotdish" will be dropped off at your door if they know you're not feeling well. People lend you their tools when you're doing one small project and investing in equipment doesn't make sense. Our tax accountant gives a pastor discount because honestly, no one is going to become a multi-millionaire serving a church, unless you become a televangelist.

There are some unusual treasures as well. After we bought our house we needed to replace the wood stove in the basement, as it's used as a primary source of heat. Not more than a few weeks later there was a knock on our door. A retired gentleman from the church grinned at me and said, "Got some firewood for you. Where can I stack it?"

Other people tell my husband they have plenty of horse manure for his vegetable garden and to "come on over any time and help yourself to it." I mentioned to him that one of these days I wouldn't be surprised if a couple of chickens and a coop showed up to keep us well fed for breakfast.

I was floored during our first Christmas at church at how people were extremely generous with gifts. Being new to the parish I thought this behavior wasn't going to last. I was wrong. Gift cards for restaurants, department stores, home stores, movie tickets and spas stacked up, year after year. Many clothes in my closet, our entire bedding set and numerous kitchen appliances have been purchased with the gift cards. Other gifts such as checks, an iPad, lumberjack-wear, and mobiles hand-made out of soda pop cans that are actually quite amazing hang from our deck. Homemade soups, cookies, candies, and desserts are unexpectedly dropped off. Quite often someone will just send us a card. "Thank you for all you do," they'll write.

Despite the tribes, despite the unhappiness with whatever someone wants to be unhappy about, despite the sanctimony, the greatest treasure is the people themselves. For every thorn in our side there are dozens of others who support and love us so much it takes away some of my cynicism about church and its politics. If I could recommend anything to those who aren't involved with a religious or spiritual group it's to seek out a community of people who can become a family to you. Don't deny yourself the treasure of a support system. No one person can be self-sufficient physically or emotionally. Even Tom Hanks had a soccer ball as his companion when he was marooned on an island in the movie *Cast Away*.

My best treasure received? A gift card to a store where I indulged myself and bought an espresso maker...cappuccinos every morning... Mmm...I still hate getting up early...

※⊛※

So many wonderful things have happened in the eight-plus years Charlie has served the church in our beautiful lake community. There are times, however, when we all feel the need to move on; when we hear that small voice telling us growth is to be found somewhere else.

Charlie and I kept our eyes and ears open and saw a curveball thrown at us.

Several months ago Charlie delivered his last sermon in this congregation and has moved onto a new call to serve as an interim pastor at another small church in a Twin Cities suburb. Word spreads quickly here. Within a week of his announcement of his resignation to the church, not just our congregation, but the entire lake community knew about it.

The very first reaction from people was, "What went wrong? Why are you leaving us?" Everyone saw this as a sudden move when in reality a pastor has usually been in the process of making a change for over a year. It takes time to discern how he or she is being led, put together that dissertation called "mobility papers," and finally, receive the call that seems to be the right place to serve for a while.

For the record, nothing went wrong. It was simply time for us, as well the congregation, to move in a different direction. The average time a Protestant minister stays at a congregation for a long-term call is seven years. Throughout our stay at this church much has changed. In some areas there has been significant growth. In other areas things have remained stagnant. Whether a pastor stays for eight years, three years or thirty years, it is ultimately the congregation's church and not the pastor's. If a congregation embraces the concept that they have ownership of their church it will continue to thrive. If the people of the church don't embrace it, the church will shut its doors.

We'll still be living in the community and no doubt will see people we know and probably on occasion will socialize with a few of them. As with any adjustment in life, I have mixed emotions. On one hand, new adventures are ahead for the two of us. I'm excited to see what the next chapter holds and what discoveries we'll make. On the other hand, I'll be leaving a group of people with whom I have become very close and there is a feeling of loss. With all new calls, it's necessary for a pastor and his or her family to sever the ties with any activity involving the former congregation. It helps bring closure, as well as making it easier for the next pastor to start fresh.

Charlie will have more difficulty than I, as he has been people's spiritual guide and will no longer be able to function in that role for them. That will be hard for so many, especially those whose lives literally depended upon his support. Some have gone through tremendous trauma and will need continual encouragement from their faith community. It's hard to let go but in many ways letting go of the familiar and comfortable are the only ways we can keep growing.

Despite being a member of this Lutheran church I don't call myself a Lutheran. When Charlie received this call nine years ago our friend Caroline asked me, "So, what does it feel like to be a Lutheran now?"

I responded, "I don't know; you tell me."

I wish I could tell everyone reading this that by marrying a Lutheran pastor I am more reassured of my faith in God, Jesus and the Resurrection.

I'm not.

In fact, I have more questions and doubts about religion and church life than I've ever had. Sometimes I become so frustrated with the Church I'd like to tear down the walls, throw out all denominations and world religions and start from scratch.

Then I tell myself, people have to start somewhere and the world doesn't need to completely reinvent the spiritual wheel.

I think back to my upbringing at St. Stephen's. It wasn't necessarily a place of immense piety. People became congregation members for various reasons. Some, because they truly believed in the Ukrainian Greek Catholic tradition, some to worship with no regard to the denomination, and some to have a family of people they could relate to.

I'm a person who falls in the last category. St. Stephen's taught me the most important lesson of this world and that is to live my life by loving and caring. Each day for me is an awkward endeavor of how I'm going to accomplish this because frankly, there are many people in this world who do and say things I don't like.

Some people wonder whether or not I am a Christian. My best answer is, it would be presumptuous of me to say I've achieved the same enlightenment as the man whom Christianity is named after. I look at the life of Jesus and marvel at what a powerful force of love he continues to be in people's lives. I'm awed by how radical and liberal he was; enough to make people think that, maybe not everything they had been taught is the correct thing to do. Something tells me that Jesus would understand my unconventional personality –not just understand, but he would encourage me to acknowledge it and live it.

As for dogma and theology, they don't influence me very much. I would be happy being a part of some sort of twelve-step program that focuses on recognizing the transgressions I've afflicted upon others, how I can rectify them, and how to bring about more love and peace in this world. I know I sound like a revolutionary hippie, but then, I come from a long line of people who have seen the worst the world has to offer and could still move forward and appreciate what they have. The Ukrainian passion and willingness to accept the best in people isn't something I can easily brush off, even when someone decides to be an ass about things.

I have the same issues as others when it comes to organized religion. The world is still hashing out whether women or homosexuals can be ordained, or can even fully participate within those specific denominations or world religions because their chromosomes don't fit the standard XY of heterosexual males. There has been sexual abuse with children and vulnerable adults that has been covered up or looked upon as being insignificant. Some dark-skinned people are called terrorists and are hated by dutiful Bible-believing, church-going groups, simply because a very small minority of individuals from a world religion outside of Christianity has an evil agenda. Other dark-skinned people are encouraged to form their own churches and not mingle with the white folks in resolutely racist communities. The more I travel and the older I get, my witness of such bigoted divisiveness has often made me feel like giving up on all religion.

Yet, for some reason, I haven't. Maybe it's because certain church congregations have meant the world to me. Maybe it's because every time Charlie gives a sermon, he speaks of how Jesus' messages have meaning in today's world if we just took the time to look at his teachings in a radically different way. And maybe it's because too many weird things have happened to me that makes me feel I'm being cared for by someone or something I can't see.

Many years ago I left college never wanting to be married to a pastor. I didn't marry a pastor – I married Charlie. Because of him I'm a better person, not because he is a pastor, but because of who he is personally. I support and encourage him and he does the same for me. We respect each other's spirituality because the end result is the same – having trust in something we can't explain and continually striving to show love and care for others.

I'd like to think I transformed the job description of The Pastor's Wife a little, or at least for some of us who don't wish to follow the traditional path.

I'll never make coffee at the right strength. I'll never lead a Bible Study. I won't be sitting in the front pew of a church every Sunday. I'll continue to do and say things that some people feel are irreverent. And I *definitely* won't be dressing like a traditional Pastor's Wife. But you know what? I'm quite okay with that and so is just about everyone else who has gotten to know me during this last call of my husband's.

At Charlie's final service I showed up in hot contrasting purples, multi-colored jewelry and my swan song accessory was my purple/pink/orange/gold-sequined shoes. Just about everyone complimented me on my apparel and said they will miss seeing me dressed up so wild and crazy for church.

There was no opinion from Jumper Lady. She left our church years ago.

So yes, I do believe people think of me as The Pastor's Wife.

Just don't introduce me as one.

Call me Talia.

Epilogue

A Conversation with the Universe

Talia: Hey there.

Universe: HEY – good to hear from you! What's up? Talk to me!

T: I'm lying in bed with Charlie. He, of course has fallen asleep within five minutes. He's doing his usual "snore-puh-puh-puh" thing when he's drowsing off.

U: Don't you usually put in the earplugs when he does that?

T: Yeah, but I'm so comfortable next to him I thought this would be a good time to talk with you.

I'm ready to go to print with the book and a lot is going on in my mind.

U: Like what?

T: The usual stuff when I'm going to launch something big and important to me. Nervousness, fear, excitement, second-guesses.

U: Well, that's to be expected.

T: The old tapes are starting to run in my head. "What if this is a stupid idea, what if what I have to say is even worth reading, you know, the 'whatifs'..."

U: Everyone has them.

T: I know.

U: So, what's the worst thing that could happen?"

T: The book really sucks and I find out I'm not good at writing.

U: And then what?

T: Well, I would be disappointed.

U: Yep, that's about it.

T: Part of my nervousness is that I've written some stuff that may be a bit controversial to some people. Some might be offended.

U: Are you intentionally looking to offend anyone?

T: No.

U: Then it's their problem, not yours.

T: *Sigh.* Y'know, it's not that easy to put yourself out on a limb, spill your guts out to total strangers and then eventually find out they might have animosity towards you.

U: Again, it's their problem. You've dealt with this before.

T: Yes, I have, and it sucks.

U: No one said saying what you honestly feel is ever popular.

T: Nope, popularity was never something I strived for.

U: Good for you for remembering that.

I'm glad we're talking again. It's been, what, fifteen years since the first time?

T: Yep. I remember the first time it happened. At first, the experience almost blew me away! And then, I was fascinated how information was flying, not just in my head, but throughout my entire body.

Out of curiosity, why did these conversations between us begin in the first place?

U: You needed some insight and you were ready to receive it this way.

T: It was a year before Charlie and I started dating, shortly after Jane died. I felt like I was smacked in the head when you told me he would be an important person in my life. When I asked in what way, why did you tell me I didn't need to know?

U: Because you didn't need to know at that time. That's all you need to know.

T: *AAHHHH!!!* Sometimes you can be so frustrating!

U: I honestly don't do it on purpose.

T: I still haven't figured out who or what you are. I call you the Universe.

U: I know you do.

I could be anything. I could be God, I could be your conscience, I could be the spirit of someone who you feel you need to talk to, or an angel. Why do you ask?

T: I just wish I could be absolutely sure of something.

U: Ha ha...nobody is absolutely sure of anything. In response to your curiosity, does it really matter who I am? And out of curiosity for me, why do *you* think you and I have conversations like this?

T: Because I always feel better when we talk.

U: Then don't sweat who I am.

T: Okay...I just want to know that someone is on my side.

U: The Universe is *always* on your side.

T: Not everyone is on my side. Some people don't like me, some I know hate me. And what about that Satan guy people like to keep talking about? Satan supposedly is not on anyone's side.

U: Satan is evil with a name attached to it. For some people it helps to have names to refer to – G-d, Satan, Allah, the Universe. The Universe is perfect in itself; people have the choice to live in an evil way and sometimes using the word Satan is the way people identify with evil that goes on in the world.

T: Just before my breakdown someone told me it was Satan that was making me feel so awful and I needed to keep praying to God to somehow "exorcise" Satan out of me. I was ready to tell her to go to hell.

U: Well, instead, you screamed at God. And you went to a hospital and got help.

T: Does a being named Satan actually exist?

U: Does it matter to you if Satan is a being or not?

T: No, not really.

U: Then there's another thing you don't need to sweat over.

T: Wait...let's go back to something you said earlier. You said the Universe is perfect. How can you even say that? Every human being on this earth is flawed.

U: What I said was the Universe is perfect and people have the choice to live in an evil way.

And what would be the purpose of living on this earth if people didn't have choices available to them?

T: No hunger, no wars, no bickering, no disease, no who is right or wrong about religion, or the way you should live.

U: Sounds kind of dull to me.

T: Well, then, *you* try living this life.

U: I do. Every moment, in every thing, I live it.

T: Don't you ever want to give up on us?

U: No! I see it this way. You're not perfect because it gives you room to grow. The beauty of imperfection is that you and everyone else can become better each day you live your life.

T: I'd like to, just once, feel a Perfect Moment.

U: Geez, Talia, you live perfect moments all the time; you just don't pay attention to them. I want you to think right now. Tell me about a time when you've felt a Perfect Moment.

T: *(Pause)* Well, let me see. There was the first time I held Irina in my arms. I'd never experienced a love like that.

U: Keep going.

T: Also, the moment in the cabin when I got pissed off at God and somehow made the decision to go seek help at a hospital. That was very painful, but it was Perfect.

U: How was it Perfect for you?

T: I realized someone else's life was more important than mine – Irina's. I also saw how everything fell into place that day with all my friends available and ready to help just at the exact time I needed it.

U: That's a rather profound Perfect Moment, I should say. Keep going.

T: When Charlie told me he didn't want me to leave after that awful brawl he and the boys had our first Christmas together.

U: You'd never been loved like that before, had you?

T: No.

U: There's still another time.

T: (*Crying*) When Dad waved his last good-bye to me.   It was the same kind of love I felt when I held Irina in my arms when she was born.

U: I was wondering when you'd cry about it.

T: I miss him so much... I miss our talks... I miss my mom.

U: Of course you do. You have the spiritual gift of conversation.

T: I do, though sometimes what I say can really piss people off.

U: Yes, it can, however you took the hard road to get to the point where you feel comfortable confronting people. You've met those tapes in your head like a warrior and are now discovering all the wonderful things you were born with.

T: But the tapes still play.

U: The tapes will *always* be there. The difference now is that you have slowly stopped listening to them. It's an ongoing process. It's part of never reaching perfection, giving you the gift of getting better and better each day.

T: But there are still days where I feel as if I'm not accomplishing anything, when depression and anxiety exhausts me, and I feel like such a sloth.

U: So, what's going to happen to this world if you decide to spend a day or a week or however long you need to on the couch, watching all seven seasons of *The West Wing?*

T: It'll go on without me. But it seems like such a waste of my life.

U: Listen – don't *ever* underestimate the things you call a waste of your life. Your down time may be something that's necessary for you to recharge for your next adventure. You're not a machine. You need time to slow down.   You need time to talk to me and reflect on it.

Let's get back to the book. Why did you write it?

T: I was bored.

U: Get out of here – really, *why* did you write it?

T: It was therapeutic for me.

U: And...

T: And, I hoped in some small way it would be therapeutic for the person reading it.

U: In what way?

T: That it's not just okay, but essential to be who we were born to be.

U: *Eureka!*

T: I don't always believe it's that simple.

U: Ah, but it is.

Tell me, do you fear life?

T: What?! That was a quick subject change!

U: I'm asking you, do you fear life?

T: Do you mean do I fear what lies ahead, or fear dying, or fear I'll fail at something?

U: All of the above. And I want you to really think about it.

T: Well, I have moments, but in general, no, I don't. Why do you ask?

U: Because in the book you talk about wishing you could be sure of your faith, or God, or what is the ultimate truth. You don't fear life because you know you ultimately can't control everything that happens to you. You've surrendered yourself to that truth, and you also know you have a choice on how you'll react to it. Even during the worst times in your life, you never once said, "I can't live this life anymore." You've always had hope to keep going.

T: It doesn't help though, when I see the ugliness that happens in this world like misogyny, or homophobia, or bigotry, or persecution or things even worse! It makes no difference how I react to a situation when there's still such a broken world.

U: Oh, but it does. You've come a long way. You've realized that no person in this world feels normal. You can sympathize as well as empathize with people and you're getting better at not getting sucked into their problems. You call people on their lies or their manipulations. And you're getting better at being diplomatic about it. You've tried to be friends with your enemies and in some cases you've seen miracles happen when your enemy has become your friend.

You can't fix anyone and you can never fix every evil going on in the world. You can only be an example to others and they'll either take the bait of compassion or they won't.

T: So, what do I do from here?

U: Keep your eyes open. You wrote this book not because you wanted it to be the next best-seller. You wrote it because your heart told you that you had something to say to the world. That it's not okay to hide things, or not to be true to yourself. That it's okay to be different from what's expected and to not conform for popularity's sake.

T: Hmm...I'll take that as a sign of support, I guess.

U: *You guess?!* Since when have you become so apathetic? You're disregarding your instincts!

T: Hey – whoever you are, I'm *trying* to understand why I'm still confused about who I am!

U: "Not try   do or do not."

T: Thanks a lot, Yoda.

U: Yoda was very wise.

Let's get back to the issue of confusion. Talk to me about it.

(Long silence)

T: Okay. You know what it is? I had all the answers when I was a kid. I knew what I believed in, and nothing changed that belief. I was told to pray for things and I expected them to happen, but they didn't. I felt screwed. I eventually worked through that entire trauma with Jillian, but I'm in this limbo world of believing and not-believing. My heart will feel one thing and a million other people with a million different opinions will tell me I'm completely wrong! Not just wrong, but that I'm going to hell for it! And I'm married to someone who, despite his fleeting doubts, can stand up in front of a group of people every Sunday and convince them that a guy named Jesus came to change the world and be our savior. I don't get it! I don't get the crucifixion and I don't know why Jesus being tortured to death somehow absolves all our sins! I've been writing for a year-and-a-half, making so many discoveries about myself and yet I'm *still* living in doubt! That shit about me having an unconventional belief system because I'm unconventional may be true, but I'm frustrated as hell! I'm afraid I'm still missing something and I want something concrete!

U: Well...okay then. You want something concrete?

T: Yes...please!!

U: Faith is not a science. You can't put it into a one-size-fits-all compartment. Turn off those tapes and listen to me for a minute.

Everyone believes in a different way. Everyone is made differently. You are you, and Charlie is Charlie, and Gandhi is Gandhi, and Buddha is Buddha, and Jesus is Jesus.

And Pat Robertson is Pat Robertson.

T: I don't like Pat Robertson! How did he get into this conversation?

U: He was mentioned because you're thinking about him. His belief system is distinctively different from yours. Every other person I mentioned you admire. I threw his name in to help you understand what you *do* believe in.

Go back and reread the chapter "Facing the Demons – Reprise" after you and I are through talking. Stick with the belief that everyone has junk and as human beings we are called to love and forgive everyone.

T: But that doesn't seem to be enough!

U: So what do you want? A Moses on the mountaintop experience?

T: It would be helpful!

U: Listen, there are people in this world who have evidence *right in their faces* about something and they'll tell you it doesn't prove anything. God could walk right through the door and someone who has never taken the time to think for themselves would say, "Hey – you're not God, that's not what was in the book of Revelation!"

Or another person would say, "There's no proof you exist, so I must be dreaming that I'm seeing you."

Just tell me this: what is something you've witnessed that has touched you so deeply and made you feel like you've never felt before? We talked about this earlier. What is it?

T: Perfect Moments. Those Perfect Moments came out of love.

U: Exactly. Remember that. Right now, forget about the semantics of religion.

Religion *has* its usefulness. Some people live by it and can't live without it. You're a person who doesn't feel pulled that way. So what? Talk to me if it helps. I'm here to tell you that you're doing fine. You're not perfect, but there's a reason for that. Embrace that unconventional personality you were born with. Stop worrying so much about someone else's beliefs. Do what you've been doing. Keep loving people.

T: I still don't like the things Pat Robertson says and what he stands for.

U: Fine. If it makes you feel better, tell him why you don't like him. If you don't think he'll listen to you, I wouldn't waste your time. Just love him.

T: That's a really hard thing for me to do.

U: I know it is. You're human.

(Long pause.)

T: Well, I'm sending this book for publication tomorrow. The die will be cast, as Julius Caesar said. I don't know if I'm lucky casting the dice of literature.

U: You know what? You already threw the dice when you decided you weren't going to take the opinions of your college professors who told you that you were an average writer. You did it anyway. You've already won the gamble.

T: Thanks. I needed that reassurance.

U: Don't mention it. I'm always here when you need me.

T: Thanks.

U: One last suggestion.

T: What would that be?

U: Call up Jillian and meet with her. There's only so much I can do. She's in your life for a reason.

T: Will do.

U: Now get some sleep. Tomorrow I want you to go to your computer and write down the conversation we've just had. It'll be your last chapter.

T: I don't suppose I should ask why.

U: You're catching on. You don't need to know. You've always trusted me.

T: Yeah, deep down, I always have.

U: Good night, Talia

T: Good night, Whoever you are.

Ideas for Reflection

1. How did your upbringing define you? What, if any traditions do you still keep and why do you continue with them?
2. Youth and adolescence is a period of time when no one feels normal. What was it that made you feel differently from others during those years? What were some circumstances that added to the discomfort?
3. As an adult, when did you feel you were not invited to be a part of a "tribe?" In what instances do you become a "tribal member?"
4. How much conviction do you have in your faith? What are your feelings regarding people of other faiths? Do you ever take part of other forms of worship or belief? Why or why not?
5. In what areas are you willing to "step outside the box" to grow and learn about yourself? In what areas do you feel less confident in discovering?
6. Do you feel you are, for the most part, your "authentic self?" Do you embrace who you are or do you find you conform to what others expect you to be?

Acknowledgements

I could have never written this book without The Pastor himself – Charlie – and my beautiful "PKs" – Irina, Troy, and Spudly. You inspire me to be a better person and I love you all very much.

Thanks to my brothers, Mike and Paul, for being a part of many of my stories and never discouraging me from trying new things in my life (at least not to my face.)

My gratitude goes out to each and every member of St. Stephen's Church Ukrainian Greek Catholic Church; you will always be my family.

I'd like to thank Jamie Cesa for challenging me to write my first chapter, to Shawn Lawrence Otto for guiding me in my pursuit as a writer, and to Cheri Register for preparing me by letting me know that to be an author takes hard, hard work.

Thanks to James Michael Larranaga for the support and resources to move forward in publishing and marketing and to my editors Chris Noel and Betsy Carlson for being my grammar and punctuation police.

Thank you, Tanya Miller, for your PR acumen and my biggest cheerleader. To Nik VanDenMeerendonk and Marino Eccher, your creativity and side-splitting humor makes work feel like play. Also, thank you to those who offered critical feedback – Bonnie, Barb, Suzi, Kris, Olena, Steve, Nik, David, Marino, Joy, Laura, LeDema, Tonya, Rebecca, Carly and Lois.

To Jillian – you are a God-send! You've helped me deal with the hard-core junk and I came out of it remarkably sane.

Finally, I wish to thank Louie and Anna, my parents, whose love and support were always my strongest foundation. I loved you in this life and continue to in whatever world you're blissfully in.